Women and Power
Gaining Back Control

by Vida Pearson

PAVIC Publications
Library & Learning Resources

Sheffield
City Polytechnic

Published by PAVIC Publications, Sheffield City Polytechnic
36 Collegiate Crescent, Sheffield S10 2BP England. Tel 0742 532380

Printed by Thomson-Shore, Inc., 7300 West Joy Road, Dexter, Michigan, 48130

First US Edition 1992
Copyright © Vida Pearson 1992

ISBN 0863392814

Cover Design by Vida Pearson and Jane Heaton

Graphics by Jane Heaton

American Edition Distributed by Inland Book Company
140 Commerce St
East Haven CT 06512
Tel (800) 243 - 0138

Acknowledgements

to individual women who have contributed to the theory and construction of this book are:

Shirley Payne, who edited and re-edited the whole volume with such dedication and skill, and who made this book a possibility.

Isobel Clarke who lent her many years of wisdom and struggle in support of the philosophical messages.

Jenny Thomas who gave emotion, energy and information, particularly for the Chapter on Dealing With Violence.

Manjeet Tara who provided inspiration, insight and support because of her struggles around power and oppression and whose work was used in the Health and Safety Chapter.

Monica Moseley who gave the opportunity for this book to be published, and steered it and us through many difficulties.

Aileen Wade and Jackie Evans for their editing skill and energy.

Jane Heaton for all the graphic design and desk-top publishing.

Judith Lowe and Isabel Wright for their generous sharing of self defence techniques from their book 'Streetwise'.

Penny Hefferan for her help and belief in Becoming Able.

Janet Robson who considerably assisted with the Knowing our Bodies and Lifting Chapters.

Anne Palmer whose ideas are interwoven in the Earth, Wind, Fire and Water Chapter and who has given constant support.

Liz Hughes and Nici Robertson who so willingly and painstakingly assisted in organising recommended reading.

The Gaining Back Control Conference workshop leaders, Marianne Skeltcher, Femi Otitoju, Lata Allman, Christine Wood, Dina Abbott, Sharon Young, Sandra Allwood and Beverley Smith, who all contributed in their support of ideas and theory.

The forty Leicester Recreation and Arts workshop leaders who contributed so much time and effort to developing theory on the practical chapters of this book and particularly Hema Vanmali, Angela Bishop and latterly Jenny Stein.

Margaret Blanksby for her innovative management ideas and for providing a reason for women to meet and discuss issues.

Celia Brackenridge whose energy has always made things move.

Diana Woodward who has always given support.

Janet Smith and Penelope Foxall for technical information on lifting and self defence.

Lynn Uriarte who believes anything might be possible.

A little bit more about the author

Vida was given life in 1952 by a working class family in Southampton. Since then, her heart has pumped 55,840,000 gallons of blood around her body. Her 656 muscles have moved her to various locations in the world including 3 years living in Philadelphia, USA, where she gained her Masters Degree in Social Policy and Planning.

After 10 years working, campaigning and living in Brent, London, she settled in Leicestershire. She spent an eventful two years with the Leicester Recreation and Arts Department as their Womens Equality Officer before freelancing as a Management Consultant and Trainer.

Quite often she sings:

> "Row, row, row your boat
> Gently down the stream,
> Merrily, merrily, merrily, merrily,
> Life is but a dream".

She enjoys saying and doing things that are a bit different.

Don't you?

WOMEN AND POWER is simply laid out and sensibly written. Its aim is to help women to take control of themselves and their situations. None of us need be victims; all of us can be strong.

Jeanette Winterson

This Book is dedicated to Julie Lydall who believed,

and to my mother, Ambuja, for teaching me.

CONTENTS

For Trainers, Educationalists and Consultants,
if you wish to use the materials in this book for your work ...

We must remind you that the Copyright, Designs and Patents Act 1988, **restricts any form of photocopying or reproduction** of the materials found in this book.

However, we have photocopying packs of selected materials on each of the chapters in the book. These are designed for use with small groups of women, in tandem with the contents of the book. They are not for re-sale.

These may be purchased from us at competitive rates.

Phone or write to: PAVIC Publications
Sheffield City Polytechnic
36 Collegiate Crescent
Sheffield
S10 2BP
England

Telephone: 01144 - 742 - 532380

Contents

Our Learning to Become Able
Growing and developing
Becoming able to the level of our ability

CHAPTER 12
TAKING RESPONSIBILITY

CHAPTER 1
FIRST WORDS

Many women have contributed to this book, knowingly and unknowingly. Over the past few years it has been reassuring and exciting to realise that there is an extremely strong 'sub-culture' of ideology amongst women in the UK. We hesitate to use words which may describe us and then label us at the same time but some of the elements of this ideology emanate from:

- a desire to seek the truth
- a desire to change inequalities
- a desire to be efficient and responsible
- a desire to understand power
- a desire to validate
- an ability to live with risk-taking

Very often women from completely different backgrounds and experiences display these values to each other. Our 'Womens Liberation Movement' on the surface appears disjointed and uncoordinated. Underneath this however, I am firmly convinced that there are many thousands of us struggling 'to make it better for us as women', in all our diversity.

The idea for this book came about because of my work as a Sports Centre Manager. In the early '80's women were not using sports facilities, aerobics had not been invented and we were labelled as 'unfeminine' 'dykes' and 'aggressive lesbians' if we wanted to be physical and strong. I soon realised that the implications of our NOT being fit, healthy and STRONG were to keep us subdued, feeling physically inferior and easy targets for oppressors. As a lesbian I was also only too aware of the terror some women feel when competing in sport in case they are labelled 'unfeminine'.

Then I put two obvious things together.

Men ARE frightened by the idea of a woman not only physically being superior to them but ALSO of women rejecting them sexually because we MAY BE lesbian.

Superficially, it seems unreal and yet it is perfectly logical.

The patriarchy keeps us in our place ultimately through physical strength and maintains this ideology by constantly telling us we are weak.

The frightening thing about being strong AND being 'out' as a lesbian is that a choice has been exercised. The individual has decided to do what the ruling group doesn't want her to do. Owning our own wants, desires, abilities and self identity, whatever they are, gives us great power.

So, in my formulating of the ideas in this book many women have provided their wisdom, displayed their stamina and illustrated their strength. They decided to move on and explore new territory because they wanted more choices in their lives.

There are particular groups of women who have made a special contribution:

- The members of the Womens Sports Foundation who are striving for equality and new values in sport - especially when we started out in 1984 and there was so much hostility against women in sport.

- Also, the women staff and the hundreds of women who have used Charteris Community Sports Centre in Kilburn, London and who, in all their diversity have PROVEN that we can develop, become stronger, more able and MOVE ON.

- So too the 250 women who were involved with me in the Conference 'A Days Step Forward' at Leicester Recreation and Arts Department when the fabric of this book was discussed and argued over, in 1988. This was an important event because women were living the problems that a male dominated industry imposed on them. The Conference was organised with the assumption that women in the Department were strong BUT were being disadvantaged by male ideology and work methods. The sharing and exchange of information, skills and experience started an initiative which expected women to work constructively in solving problems.

  The commitment shown by the women displayed their overwhelming eagerness to become more able in the work they were doing. They generally wanted to find their own methods of how to deal with aggression and harassment, how to lift heavy equipment and how to challenge unsafe work practices.

- This valuable thinking was further explored at the Gaining Back Control Conference organised by Re-Source in 1990. This national seminar provided an opportunity for women to think positively about dealing with aggression and racial and sexual harassment, self defence, managing stress, lesbian strength, becoming able, being outdoors and health and safety.

- Another influence on the structure and theory of this book came from two 'Framework' Conferences for women involved in Women in Management Education. A small group of us who are concerned about management practice in Britain organised the meetings in 1989. It was there that participants placed very clear emphasis on our learning to take responsibility for our power and our values. They went further to suggest that these qualities are fundamental to management practice and until individuals live and work them there will always be exploitation.

  Characteristically for gatherings of women, the emphasis in all the exchanges and deliberations was to start first with ourselves and work outwards from there.

That is where this book begins and also ends.

In between there is reference to and examination of how we are made powerless and affected by circumstances, but the central theme is that of self-empowerment.

It has been important to work from a vision of how we might be. This vision has been constructed by bringing together strands of thought and experience with which we are all familiar. It is apparent in this capitalist patriarchy that we live disjointed and distracted lives. We are constantly bombarded by bits of information and knowledge and are kept bewildered at the level of operation - having to respond to male ideology and demands. The selection of ideas in the vision have come through our struggles as women and have been put into a holistic framework. It is posed merely as a means for starting discussion, debate, argument and controversy.

Many of us do not like the values and ideology we are forced to live with. Amidst all this we are creating new expectations of behaviour - especially through assertiveness training. These skills and wisdoms are women-made and their different approach and values should be validated and owned by us. Unless we have some structure and expectation of what we want for ourselves we will never grasp our abilities to change what is wrong and to think forward in terms of major societal change.

The kind of society we want to live in is the kind of society which we would like to live in our personal lives. We know that we cannot achieve anything unless we believe we want something to be different.

The ideas in this book give practical hints, techniques and methods of assuming and assessing the powers we all individually own. The intention has been to keep the ideas as bare as possible and the layout of the book attempts to leave space for the reader's own thoughts.

The ambition is to put it all together so that we recognise our fundamental rights about the way we, and others, use power.

The figure on the next page illustrates the vision which encapsulates the messages in this book....

Figure 1

Vision
The Physically and Emotionally Assertive Woman Is

Aware
Whole
Strong

Physically   Emotionally

Constantly searching for
Knowledge

Abilities   Attitudes

Able to use resources   **Understands outcomes**
creatively and satisfactorily

Able to make decisions based on knowledge
and confidence in an owned future

Using her power to protect her own self esteem and self esteem of others

The Book Outlined

The central pivot in gaining strength and power is in acquiring, having, being in control of and owning knowledge. Since we have been restricted by men in knowledge, the message hinges on the understanding and growth of knowledge of our physical capacity as women, from our point of view.

We explore first, the emotional sides of assertiveness and then move on to the physical areas of concern which can help equip us in becoming stronger women.

Our attitude psychologically is challenged in the early chapters and then later we consider methods and techniques to enable us in acquiring physical presence.

> **Here, the emphasis is on building ability.**

We may have the knowledge stored up in our brains but, unless we tell ourselves we CAN become stronger and then learn techniques and become able, we are still disadvantaging ourselves.

The Chapters Outlined

Knowing Power

There are many reasons for our being limited in knowing ourselves physically and emotionally but fundamentally it is because power relationships in a western and white patriarchal society are *based* in the physical ability of the ruling group to coerce and control.

If a woman knows her own power she may wish to re-arrange a few things about the house! The work place! The country!

Before anything else understanding the **sources of power** puts oppression into a framework of reasons. To understand how power is created is to begin to understand our own power.

The concept of power has been so distorted that we are led to believe that the *observation* of power is power itself. We observe an authoritarian personality and believe that person to be powerful. This is a fallacy. They are only powerful IF they have a SOURCE of power. Inevitably, their source of power will be based in the physical ability to dominate.

In this chapter we take a completely new look at the concept of power. Power is everything and therefore writing about it could be endlessly technical and obscure. This chapter attempts to put forward, in as simple a picture as possible, a renewal of understanding about where we get our power from.

It comes first because the rest of the book hangs from it.

Knowing Our Fears

One method of maintaining power relationships is through the ruling group wielding tools of threat. These threats are nurtured in our fears.

Significantly, our bodies respond to fear and the physical response often dictates our emotional response.

Unless we know what our own personal fears are we will never truly grasp our potential to overcome them and for becoming physically and emotionally strong.

Management of Stress

The emotional bridge between fear and power is understanding stress and how it affects and controls us in undesirable ways.

However, it can also be used positively to our own benefit.

Stress management is therefore fundamental in today's high speed, high stress life.

Living Assertively

Assertiveness training is now a very popular means of identifying desirable and undesirable behaviour. It has given us tools to criticise constructively ourselves and others.

We take another look at assertiveness however, and question what the dangers are as well as reviewing the benefits.

Knowing Our Bodies

We need to be continuously aware of how our bodies work mechanically because through this we become conscious of the physical limits we can subject them to.

If we understand how our body works we know better how to care for it, energise it and maintain it. Further, we are better informed in knowing how much stronger we can become.

Knowledge also reminds us that we may mis-use our body, that we are subjecting it to intolerable strain or abuse. Understanding how our body works is to provide further choices in the way we conduct our every day life.

Protect Your Back - Lift It!

No matter what we lift from the floor upwards, it will be heavy. Gravity wants to pull the object down again. Our ability to lift any thing is dependent on two factors - our strength and our technique.

Understanding how we can lift heavy items through knowledge of technique both empowers us and protects our first resource - our body.

Our comprehension of the mechanics we are using when lifting and carrying objects will keep us firmly in control, knowledgeable of what we realistically can or cannot achieve.

Many sports facilities have fitness and weights rooms and women should feel easy and free to use them. The last part of this chapter introduces the reader to the use of a weights room.

Earth, Wind, Fire and Water

One of the most tragic losses in human experience, in the so called 'civilised' world is that of being separated from the elements and the power of the earth, wind, fire and water.

The twentieth century phenomenon of capitalist wealth is that of shelter, protection, warmth, food and overbearing control of the physical environment, whereas our survival through the ages has depended upon humans living and learning methods to cope with the environment which has usually been hostile.

Re-learning the challenge of outdoor living re-awakens our weaknesses and strengths in the context of forceful, environmental reality.

'Health and Safety' - From a Woman's Point of View

The man-made physical environment has been designed by men with men in mind. 'Health and Safety' relates nearly always primarily to the health and safety of men.

We are entitled to review our environment and consider how it can actually dictate against us and keep us intimidated. Our working and living conditions affect our welfare. We can have opinions about this. They need to be informed and sturdy.

Dealing with Violence or Its Threat

Having understood a vast background of physical comfort and ease of behaviour there may be times when skill in self defence will help maintain confidence under threatening circumstances.

Recognising what is violence and what is aggression is essential.

Self defence techniques rely on a wide range of actions which may be available to a woman under threat. Her survival under extreme threat is paramount and is not only dependent on her physical reactions but also her analysis and intuition. Some straight forward physical reactions to attack can make the difference, this chapter puts forward a few basic but easily understood guidelines.

Becoming Able

Too frequently we cannot bear to acknowledge our disabilities. To do so is to accept the prevailing notion that somehow we have failed in some way or other. It is also to accept that part of us may never be 'right' again, may never function in the way it should.

We can talk ourselves into thinking that we really are 'whole' human beings when in fact hardly any soul on earth can match up to that perfect specimen so insidiously promoted by the male media. But, they give us a double message because not only are we to be perfect sexual and reproductive beings for men, we are also to be 'weak' - weaker than men.

From this stance the picture becomes clearer. ALL of us need to turn around and consider our disability. And ALL of us can move towards becoming able *to the level at which we individually define our ability*.

Some of us are more distinctly and clearly 'disabled', but the essence here is that we can work with what we have, develop it and build on the difficulties and disadvantages this materialistic society imposes upon us.

If it moves we CAN move it better!

Taking Responsibility

Often, to take responsibility is to decide positively about a future action. We make decisions having thought out many and varied factors.

To wield power over someone else or over many people is something which women may either shy away from or try to evade. Perhaps it is because women have been too much at the brunt end of others wielding power over them? Whatever - this chapter expects the individual to be responsible for her actions by noting that virtually ALL action is powerful in some way or another.

A certain morality shines through here because it is assumed that the individual endeavours not only to build choices for herself, but that she is also prepared for consequences. They may or may not be 'good' or 'honourable' consequences but, the responsible individual is thoroughly aware of her vast potential for being 'in control' rather than 'controlling' or 'being controlled'.

Our abilities to be physically and emotionally assertive women are grossly under-used at present. This book draws attention to the many ways of developing our strengths.

The contents pages provide a breakdown of each chapter so that the book may be used as a manual. However, the fabric and theme constantly returns and runs throughout. It is good to pursue it because then strength is gained through understanding knowledge from many different view points.

The reader may wish to return to some chapters because initially they may appear strange or unfamiliar. This may be particularly the case for the Chapter Knowing Power.

CHAPTER 2
KNOWING POWER

What is Power?

Movement is power.

Because of movement there is change.

We need energy to move.

The source of all our natural energy is the sun.

The sun is all-powerful.

The sun gives energy.

We use this energy to move.

We too have power.

The constant theme throughout this book is this:

> **If we are alive we have energy.**
>
> **If we use our energy we move.**
>
> **If we move we become powerful.**
>
> **Understanding power gives us choices.**

To bring some simplicity to a subject of extreme complexity we take an overview in this chapter of the two major sources of power in our lives:

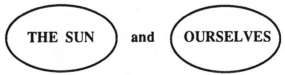

Unless we understand the sources of power we cannot hope to comprehend ways of better using our power.

Examining the power of the sun asks us to question how we mimic that power.

It is timely to be reminded of how humanity is so dependent on the sun and its power. We may be miniscule, insignificant creatures, but we live because of the sun and because of all its effects.

The concept of power has been distorted because we too often look at the EFFECT of power and not at the SOURCE of power.

To help us to understand the difference between the two we shall examine how the sun is THE source of power to humanity. Then, we consider how we as individuals are also sources of power.

> **It has been very convenient for powerful people to encourage our forgetting the power of the sun.**

Re-collecting our knowledge of the sun's power allows us to realise how much we take from the sun. It is because of that taking that we are alive and powerful now.

Realising the nature of the sun's power provides us with a framework from which we can identify our own power. It also suggests a means of identifying the power of other people. We shall therefore examine the characteristics of the sun and its effects on the earth. After this we shall explore how we, as tiny replicas of the sun, can mimic its power. Through this comparison we are then able to comprehend better how some people **are** more powerful than others.

The picture of the sun and ourselves as power sources displays the main features of the rest of the book, see Figure 2 on pages 12 and 13.

It is expected that the book will challenge us to reconsider the way we use our own personal energy and power. This theoretical background therefore provides hooks on which to hang the importance of the various elements in becoming powerful.

Power Source - The Sun

The Sun Gives Energy

The sun is powerful because it gives energy.

The heat provides the correct temperatures for life on earth which is so complicated even now we do not fully understand every facet of growth and decay.

The light offers processes for plants to photosynthesise and produce greenery. Because there is plant life, we animals feed on both plants and other animals which have eaten vegetation. Quite obviously, without heat and light we'd all die eventually. Food would run out and without heat the planet would become so hostile we'd all end up as frozen ice blocks.

> The sun has been generous over time.
>
> Through millions of years creatures and plants have grown and died and now we burn their remains away in a matter of seconds. Oil, gas, coal, the major sources of fossil energy and therefore human wealth, have all been given - endlessly.

We assume the sun has LIMITLESS energy and we then take it for granted that it will always be there.

We have forgotten how dependent we are on its generosity and take relentlessly from its power AS IF IT WERE OUR OWN.

We have also made use of fossil fuel to transform it into another form of energy - electricity. This very useful power imitates the sun by providing heat and light, but is completely controllable.

> Clean electricity.
>
> Sanitised 1990's power which flows quietly while you sleep and can be measured out just when and how you want to use it.
>
> At your fingertips.

To have the use of electricity is to have the use of power.

- Voyager II, the spacecraft which ventured to the outer zones of the solar system to Neptune has provided us with enough information to know how precariously the earth is situated in its orbit of the sun. Four and a half thousand million miles away Neptune seethes under a mass of frozen methane gas, 55 degrees below zero - because the sun's heat cannot reach that far.

Perhaps it is time to re-awaken the humble behaviour of sun worship. Maybe then we would more suitably match our taking from the sun with a real understanding of the sun's power.

The Sun Shapes the Environment

Since the sun provides heat and light, its power then affects the elements and chemicals around us.

> Our climates are totally dependent on the sun's rays and on the process of day and night.

With the given tilt of the planet the angles of the sun produce winters and summers. The weather affects everything. Too much heat produces drought, preventing plant life, giving rise to dust bowls and deserts. Too much cold creates glaciers, icecaps and lowers the sea level. The daily battle between hot and cold produces moisture and too much water makes for floods, some of which can destroy and re-shape whole landscapes.

Figure 2   **SUN GIVES**

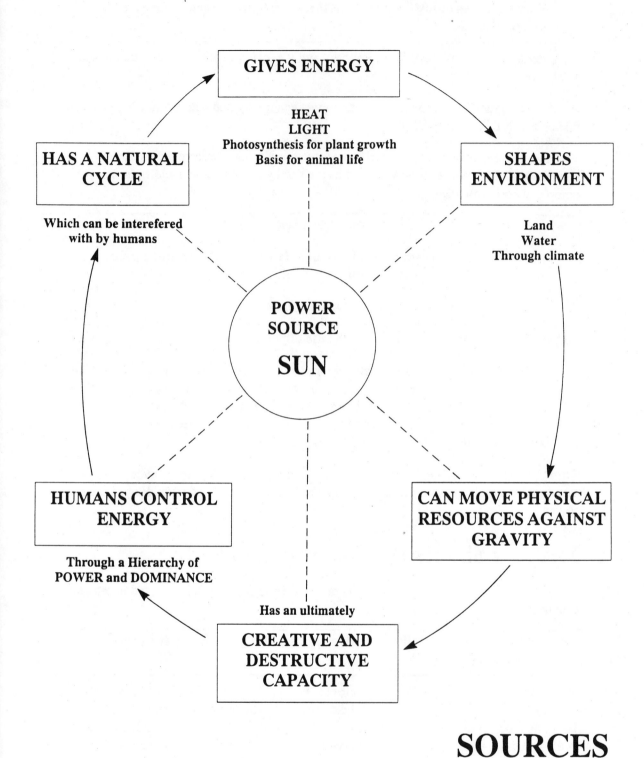

WOMAN TAKES

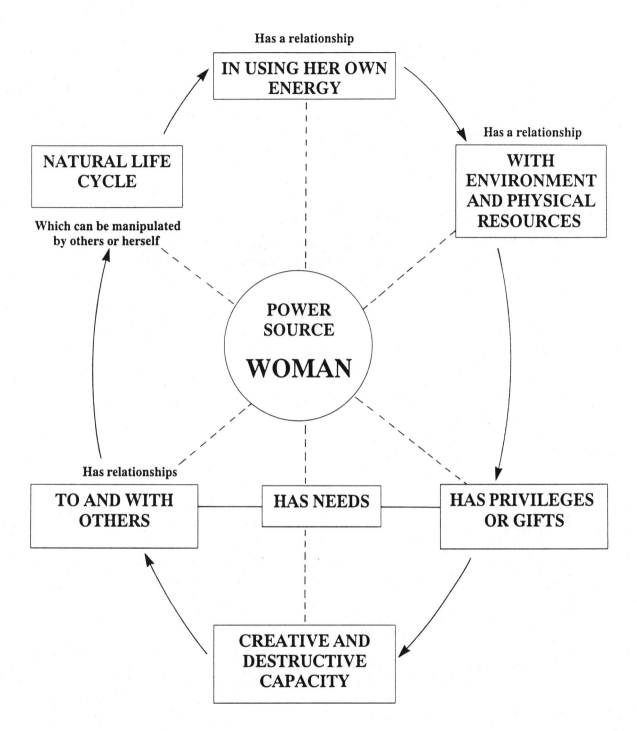

Has a relationship

IN USING HER OWN ENERGY

Has a relationship

WITH ENVIRONMENT AND PHYSICAL RESOURCES

NATURAL LIFE CYCLE

Which can be manipulated by others or herself

POWER SOURCE WOMAN

Has relationships

TO AND WITH OTHERS

HAS NEEDS

HAS PRIVILEGES OR GIFTS

CREATIVE AND DESTRUCTIVE CAPACITY

OF POWER

The weather shapes the environment continuously, especially through erosion. The physical world is an ever changing place and with no human intervention would continue breaking-down and re-constructing in a natural cycle. There would be new environments constantly being created, providing new habitats for life and old environments being ruthlessly destroyed.

The Energy of the Sun Moves Physical Resources

The power of the sun is so great that its influence moves physical resources against GRAVITY.

- The life the sun creates in trees produces pressures which draw water UP from their roots to feed and sustain branches which may be hundreds of feet high.

- A flood will carry with it masses of tons of debris perhaps hundreds of miles to the sea. Tides and currents can then take over to further fragment and disperse matter.

The earth is in orbit of the sun's gravity. We are stuck to this planet because of the earth's gravity. Gravity provides a resistance against which all movement struggles. Only energy can move something against gravity.

Electricity can be provided through the energy of the sun and this can move matter against gravity.

> **It is incredible to think that man-made nuclear power not only simulates the energy of the sun and may be used in a controllable electricity form but also that it is potentially totally destructive.**

This form of power, used by humans, takes an unprecedented step away from the millennia of earth's natural dependence on the sun.

The Sun has a Natural Cycle

The orbit of the world around the sun gives us a natural cycle which life has relied on since the first bacteria. In this second of time humanity is perilously close to interfering with the natural movement of gases and atmosphere which protect us from the harmful radioactive rays of the sun.

- The so-called greenhouse effect is merely a change in climate across the world - which may have disastrous effects on humans.

- The damaging of the ozone layer will actually interfere drastically with the very nature of chemical composition on the earth. It could be irrevocable.

Men's nuclear armouries could blow us into smithereens. It is a bleak picture.

> **Why have white men taken us all this far?**
>
> The sun shines on regardless.
>
> The earth keeps on spinning.
>
> But, in their attempt to control their environment
> men have manipulated the effects of the sun's
> natural cycle.
>
> It seems that if men can't control the very sun itself, they
> will resort to destroying the earth instead.

Humans Control Energy

The survival of the human race has depended upon the ability of the species to adapt to the environment, sometimes against hostile odds. To maintain that adaptation, men in the last two centuries (especially in the west) have controlled energy to provide greater comforts against the environment.

> **The control of energy is the control of power.**

Given that using power means something can move, ENERGY is the means by which it happens. The sun's gifts of energy are controlled by a very small number of men. Oil barons, coal and electricity boards, and governments and capitalists. These few 'big' people protect their own interests first.

They use energy through a hierarchy of power and dominance over vast numbers of people. The 'smaller' you are the smaller amount of energy you get to control.

> **The reason for controlling energy is simple.**
>
> **Without it you cannot move resources.**

Men have made themselves into miniscule suns and are constantly moving resources to benefit themselves. This small minority are able personally to hoard and control greater and greater empires of physical resources. Their ability to control other people's energy seems colossal.

There is a hierarchy of power and dominance in the world, but it is dependent on us all subscribing to it.

The Creative and Destructive Sun

To return to the sun puts our power into context however.

> **In the end the sun will win.**
>
> **It will be there far, far longer than we will.**
>
> **It has to be the ultimate answer in power.**

This is because it is intrinsically capable of both destroying and creating. It may have given the world its rich resources of life and energy but at the same time it can and will take from us, everything. One day out in the middle of the Sahara would be enough to convince anyone of that.

> **The sun is ruthless.**
>
> **All power has the potential for ruthless destructiveness.**

Without hesitation a human will die if left in an exposed place for too long - from cold or heat. We have forgotten too easily how the sun or its effects will destroy, because we have done so much to counteract the more extreme effects in the short term.

We know how friendly the sun can be because we have so much of life to benefit from its constructive capacity.

> **Our sun gives us life. It also takes it.**
>
> **All real power has the same intrinsic capacity over its field of influence to create or to destroy.**

Turning to the second part of the model we come to you, the powerful woman, also a microcosm of energy given by the sun.

We'll forget the men for a while. They hinder us too much when we come to defining our real power.

The next meal you eat will have been given by the sun. The energy you hold intrinsically as your own replicates the characteristics of the sun. That energy must go somewhere.

> **Think of yourself as a miniature sun for a short while, and explore ......**

Power Source - Woman

Looking at Ourselves as Powerful - The Powerful Woman

Each of us is a power house of energy. It may not feel like that. Indeed, some mornings it might just all seem better to lie quietly in bed rather than have to face the day. However, we do have energy. No matter how little it is, if we are alive and breathing we will always have at our disposal some energy

> Any movement we make relies clearly on the use of energy.

Some of us certainly have more available to us than others. Even so, the most important fact here is that we do have a variety of energy sources. The problem is that some lie dormant while other more pressing survival needs are met.

Sit back however, and think of the many forms energy can take in us. For example:

FORMS OF HUMAN ENERGY

Muscular energy	The energy of joy, exhilaration and hope
Resting energy	The energy of depression
Activity energy	The energy of uplifting
Electrical energy	The energy of love
Thinking energy	The energy of hatred
Feeling energy	The energy of anger
Inspirational energy	The energy of our soul
The energy of sorrow, disaster and crisis	

You will have other examples also.

At this point however, our first point of call is to accept and identify with our muscular energy. This is where all our movement originates.

> **Muscles act as a catalyst for all action.**

The very least movement we make is directed by the strength of a muscle. There are 656 muscles in the human body. We think more of their use in the chapter on lifting but at this juncture let us first accept that our bodies house vast quantities of energy, much of it stored, ready for muscular action.

- We know of courageous people who have come to terms with paralysis of major muscles but who still use what energy is available to them, TO CARRY ON LIVING. They refuse to be stuck and immobilised and use the energy at their disposal to paint pictures with their mouth muscles, play the piano with their toes or become eminent professors in mathematics using their fingertips with a computer.

Where there are muscles available to us,
food to eat,
there is energy and hope.

A Woman has a Relationship with the Use of Her Own Energy

As women we are given messages, conditions, punishments and expectations about how we use our energy, or our own power, throughout life. We have written and read countless reams on it. We have talked and spoken countless words, sometimes in whispers, other times bellowing across valleys, cities and conurbations. We are worried by it, challenged and inextricably wound up in it. And in all this we writhe, subjugated by the ruling interests around us.

"THEY are so much more powerful than ME."

"I can't do it".

"It's too much for me".

We may have had all these multitude of hazards to live through but even so, STILL we make choices about how to use our energy.

We have a relationship with our energy which walks and talks with us all day long. The little voice giving numerous instructions would get nowhere if there were not a willing organism to carry them out. Your relationship with your own energy or power level defines how you will use it.

- If you have a negative expectation of how you will use your energy you give yourself no options to use it creatively.

- If you think positively you will expect to do as you want. If you think realistically you will measure what you are ABLE to do with your knowledge of the circumstances you are in AND the energy levels you have in your body. You may be 90 years old, but if you have the wisdom of your age based on knowing these elements, you will still be active in SOME FORM OR OTHER.

This is the first premise because without it we get lost and once again forget our innate powers. All the constraints, burdens and anguish of every day life pound us mercilessly.

"It is depressing.
It is bewildering.
It is cruel.
How can anyone have any energy (enthusiasm) when it is all so gloomy?"

When we get to this place we begin our knowledge of how we can depress our own energy levels. We go down to depths of despair because energy seems to have left us. We feel utterly powerless.

Some will die feeling that way.

This is the mind living its relationship with energy.

We *feel* depressed. We *believe* we are depressed (for lots of good reasons no doubt). We don't seem to be able to *move out* from our depression. We *forget* how many other sources of energy we have available to us.

Remember, for a minute, the times in your life when the surge of action and hope have combined to fill your body with messages,

"I want to do that".

The moment of enthusiasm expects your body to respond. Understanding the connection between what motivates you and your body response starts the discovery of REALLY what you are capable of doing. The doing will use energy. Energy is power.

The Chapter Managing Stress gives information and suggestions on how to break-out of depression.

Environment and Physical Resources

So, here's a woman with a whole lot of energy and what will she do with it? To make her really powerful she will use the resources she has around her. She will move them from place to place to arrive at combinations of activity which provide her with a satisfaction of her desire.

- She puts water in the kettle for a cup of tea. She has access to another energy source - electricity - turns it on and the water heats. She does all this within the context of an environment which she also uses.

Our energy and power can change the nature of our surroundings. What the twentieth century has done in the western world however, is to make our environment so artificial that we have lapsed into a cotton wool escape from the elements. The way we use the environment is powerful because we restrict ourselves if we do not know how to survive.

Different Perceptions of Environment

1. Around your body

The environment we are most familiar with is that closest to our own body. It is our own personal space. We put on clothes to protect that personal territory. We also position ourselves in relation to the rest of the space around us.

- For instance, it might mean placing the foot well into the step as you go up the stairs, or just on the edge. Sitting nervously on the corner of a chair or deeply into it. Arms akimbo as you stand in your kitchen or small and indecisive as you tremble at the washing up.

Your personal space extends into the environment. How we want to be seen or perceived usually defines how we use our personal space. Women who think big often take a lot of personal space even to the extent that others may think them taller than they really are.

2. Living area

Where you live and how you live is often an environment which is very familiar. The feelings you have about that place may vary from being very knowledgeable of its every facet, to feeling quite disinterested in it.

- The woman who sleeps in a cardboard box may well use all her knowledge of the place she chooses to put it, to raise the chances of her surviving the night.

- The woman who is disinterested in her living area may have so many aids and resources available to make her feel secure and comfortable that she does not have the necessity to survive through knowledge. She may of course feel disinterested because it is an unhappy place to be and she will survive it regardless of her feelings because she HAS to.

Whatever you think about your living environment it is usually important to most of us. It is also an area we have personal access to for a given length of time.

3. Walking or personal movement area

All of us have an environment within which we can personally move. It may be thoroughly restricted because of imprisonment or illness so that the personal movement area is virtually the same as the living area. Or, it may be a very wide territory which could spread over many square miles.

> **How far do you personally move or independently propel yourself each day?**
>
> If your council has provided you and your community with ramps you may be able to move independently quite some way in your wheelchair.
>
> If you walk, how far do you go? To the shops? In the park? To work?
>
> How many miles do you walk at work, to go to all those meetings, the canteen or the toilet?
>
> If you cycle, what are the limits you feel comfortable with and how confident are you in using the environment you cycle in?
>
> Do the conditions change in your environment so that darkness for instance may restrict you?

Your personal movement areas are probably those you are familiar with. Opening up new areas for you to move into through exploration not only strengthens your leg or arm muscles (if you are in a wheelchair), it also opens up new possibilities of your using your energy to learn more about the environments in which you are best able to perform. Making familiar your personal movement area allows you to use it, have a relationship with it and expand your options.

What can you offer it, what can it offer you? It is YOURS TOO.

> **The sense of being part of your environment
> makes it feel like it is part of you too.**

This is explored further in the Chapter Health and Safety.

4. Travelling area

The environments you use by travelling through them are also familiar to you, but only as you see them through the window of a bus or car, train or aeroplane.

We are dependent on an engine to propel us through perhaps a rich array of environments. In effect we are protected FROM the environment by the boxes we sit in to move us.

> **Our expectation of those environments may be disproportionately based in lack of knowledge or familiarity.**
>
> **We again forget that without the moving box we may be left abandoned and helpless.**

How you respond to the underlying lack of familiarity will define your attitude to the environment as you pass through it.

How we use our energy or power in relation to the environment we are in is dependent on how comfortable we feel with it. Many of us are completely out of touch with surviving in an unkindly outdoors. The Chapter Earth, Wind, Fire and Water relate information and techniques to help us become quickly familiar with our environment, and if needs be, survive it.

Physical Resources

Every environment we use furnishes us with resources of some sort or another. We take the availability of cheap resources so much for granted that it is easy to become indifferent to their provision.

Generally speaking, the richer we become the more confident we are in using resources AS A MEANS OF BEING POWERFUL.

However, the poorer we are the more we have the opportunity to value those few resources we have. If we know what it is like to not have shoes, to not have enough to eat, to not have full health, we are more likely to put full value on attaining any of those resources.

> **By valuing a resource we put ourselves in the context of our USING it.**
>
> **We realise that if we do not have it, we cannot do what we WANT to do.**

When the car breaks down we know then how valuable it is. Using a car allows personal power far greater possibilities. Already your environment boundaries have grown out of all possible muscle power proportion. Not having the car leaves a driver stranded - a rather pathetic creature in the eyes of the woman patiently standing in the queue waiting for the No.52 bus.

Being dependent on physical resources puts us in a relationship with that resource. We allow a resource to have power over us if we do not put it in its rightful place in the world. You use the resource for certain reasons, quite plausible to yourself.

"The material I bought yesterday will be perfect for that blouse I want to make".

- You will use the resources efficiently, with as little waste as possible, to make something you feel you need. You have a good reason to have a new blouse. You need to be warm in the winter. You are familiar with how to change the material into a blouse and you will use your energy and ability to complete the task powerfully.

Having the knowledge and the ability to use resources lends you power. You can put things into places you never dreamt of once you have resources available to you, and you have the energy and motivation to do it.

What resources are you familiar with using?

The variety and quantities we have access to are mind boggling:

Flour, sugar, water, protein, furniture, toilet paper, pottery, steel, roof tiles, washing machines, microchips, aluminium, the list is almost endless.

What you are used to using defines the activity you are able to pursue.

- If you have not been taught or had experience in cooking it will take a big personal struggle to overcome lack of confidence as an adult.

- If you have never handled a spanner or a saw you may feel frightened by the power the tool has. Why should an inanimate object have such an influence?

It is what we might do with it that's the problem. You might chop your finger off with a saw or just mangle up the bike wheel completely if you exert too much force on the nuts and bolts. Or you just may look a fool.

The way you perceive a resource will specify what happens next.

There's a shelf. There's a drill. There are the brackets. They sit there. You look at it.

"I can't put it up/don't know how to/not my job to do it/better find a carpenter".

It all continues to sit there because you've no money for a carpenter. Your perception has blocked your using the tools and resources. You deny yourself the opportunity to try.

To get over the block try:

> Picking it all up
> Looking at it all over
> Feeling it
> Experimenting with positions for the shelf
> Plugging in the drill
> Reading a book about it
> Asking someone who knows

That process is familiar. Stay with what you are familiar with to extend experience and knowledge into the unfamiliar. Try using your energy differently by moving resources around. In your hands, with a tool, with a computer, with a tractor.

Our caution helps us to value the resources we are using. Our fundamental belief that waste is wrong helps us preserve a resource for future use.

Privileges or Gifts

Being perfectly honest with yourself how long was the list of resources available to you?

How often have you passed by a book and not looked in it?

How many times have you slept on your bed and is it comfortable?

Those with no sight know how valuable looking in the book is.

Those with a bad back and no money know how much a good mattress could help them - if they have been informed.

> **What makes the difference between one woman having vast quantities of resources and another very few?**
>
> **Quite simply, it is privilege.**
>
> **And yet,**
> **We are proverbially naked at birth**
> **and the same when we die.**

In between birth and death we use our energy and power to control resources. All the materials we have at our disposal are mere objects of time. In a flash they could be taken from us. Anything could happen. The earth could heave in a major quake. Our cities may be drowned as the glaciers melt.

> **Those of us who have choice through money**
> **and resources to aid us**
> **have been given gifts.**

We might feel entitled to them because we 'earned them' or slightly embarrassed because we inherited them.

> **Whatever the reason for having resources it all amounts to the same:**
>
> **The earth gave it.**
>
> **The sun helped it along.**
>
> **We are very used to taking.**

The consumer society is busily eating away at the fabric of the planet and still westerners think it a pre-ordained right of superiority to use, use, use. Our consumerist habits have made us become spoilt children dependent on the very things that are meant to help us. The so-called 'waste' from using resources is threatening our very existence and yet still we believe we have sacred rights to our material wealth.

In this competitive society we are imbued with constant propaganda to measure our lack of resources as a deficiency.

> **Why do we look at what men have when we women are so rich ourselves?**
>
> Do we think too often:
>
> "The men have so much more - and therefore they are so much more powerful."

Why have we let them maintain their power in such a way? If it came to it, could we women close down a nuclear power station, dispose of its radioactive poisons in a safe, long-term method AND provide power for the nation? We cannot criticise unless we are prepared to do the most difficult jobs. We could use the privileges now bestowed upon us to look forward to a society which uses its resources carefully and with respect.

However, unless we are completely honest in the way we view the gifts we use we will never genuinely know how to build a society free from greed. Money is merely a measurement.

> **If we put the factors together, money becomes power :**
>
> Available energy + resources = power
>
> The more money we have, the more we can choose to own energy and resources, the greater the power.

The choices we have available to us define the extent of our privilege. It is assumed here that we all have more choices than we think. They could be limitless if we are knowledgeable of consequences and of how we use resources.

This book provides an information base from which to make some of those personal decisions.

Women Have Needs

Our existence depends on our acquiring and owning resources (or gifts) which aid us in our lifestyle. What is 'necessary' for our 'survival' has been left to an individualistic market economy to define.

We are pumped daily with suggestions about what we NEED to make life so much easier. Such needs can be never ending. Motivation to survive gets mixed up with greed. If our needs are constantly defined by ruling interests it makes it hard for us to stand back and consider what we DO need.

"I need a car because I have to travel to work in it."

"I need a good music system because then I can relax"

"I need alcohol because then I can relate more easily to others".

We usually do have serious and well thought out rationale for the satisfaction of our own needs. The things around us give us comfort and an easier way of life.

Can a need be measured?

- It is clear that a woman who is unable to walk has a far greater need for a car than one who is ambulant. A resource like a car then makes the difference between a life which may be isolated and dependent on others to one of personal choice.

Taking some time to re-consider what really is NECESSARY in our lives allows us the opportunity to re-examine our relationship with the resources we depend on. We find that a need itself becomes powerful in our lives. That then becomes a reason for our activity and the way we use our energy or power.

A review of what our primary needs are helps us to put real value on resources around us and therefore to measure what is most important. We will all personally have our own priorities but here are some indicators to think over:

There is a:	
Human need to move:	The different parts of the body From one place to another To carry and use objects
To survive:	Food, water, shelter, clothing
To have protection:	Against the hostility of the environment or attack by other living creatures
To have comfort:	Which makes life easier and may give circumstances for greater production
To have community:	People together can satisfy the above needs more efficiently. There are also the gregarious needs of dependence, bonding and self worth.

Have our western 'needs' gone berserk? What measure can we use to evaluate what is fundamental?

If we are privileged enough to have choices in owning and using resources one measure of our personal need is our dependency on them. Another is to examine what our honest response would be to losing what we already have. If there is a resource that you really want because you know it will open up choices and a more satisfactory lifestyle you have an opportunity to know beforehand how valuable it is.

Our Relationships with Others

We exist as an individual placed in a hierarchy of power and dominance. We are cogs in wheels, interdependent and yet heaped on top of one another.

The whole system relies on people assuming that some individuals' needs are 'more important than others'. Social relations in a class-bound society are riddled with personal expectations of who is more superior and therefore more eminent than 'lesser beings'.

These assumptions have been used by ruling class interests to rationalise exploitation of the colonial empire. They are evident in all forms of racism. We, who benefit from the resources brought to us from other nations at hugely under-priced value, are in no position to cry crocodile tears.

> **We take copper for electricity from Latin America.**
>
> **We benefit from the labour and yield of other nations.**
>
> **Without copper most of our electrical appliances would be useless.**
>
> **We women would feel even more powerless without electricity.**

If Latin American nations were more powerful they might stop the easy availability of copper for the west. WE depend on it. If the Latin American nation were to stop production of copper the west would retaliate with great FORCE.

Let us therefore define power:
All real power has the intrinsic and ultimate ability to change the availability, more or less, of certain options or resources for another individual(s).

Ultimate, dominant power always depends on the capacity to damage another individual physically if he or she does not comply.

> **Generally, women know the effects of power more than we know or understand the sources of power.**

Power balances

The use of our energy is constantly constrained or encouraged by others. These people will be powerful in our lives.

Our relationships continually pivot in power balances. This therefore means that you are part of the balance and that you *are* powerful whether you recognise it or not. Even if you are completely subjugated by the power of another person, *they* still need *you* to continue their power base.

There are no soft options on the ultimate use of power. If power provides a forum for change then this may be beneficial or cruelly destructive.

Perhaps it depends from which side of the fence you look at it.

Much of our activity is within the context of prescribed rules and understanding of behaviour. Everything is fine until you step outside the 'norm' and behave oddly or differently.

- The reactions of other people are often determined by the interests they have in keeping the old rules.

  If you step outside too much you will either be punished or forced back into the fold.

  You will be helpless against the power of the community at large.

Attitudes and values

The balances of power rely on the expectations of the individuals concerned. Giving power or enforcing it is usually illustrated by the attitude of those involved in the balancing act.

It is therefore understandable that campaigners against racism and sexism, or any other form of oppression, usually go straight for the 'attitude' when criticising oppressors. In the same way that someone who is different is often labelled as having 'an attitude'.

> **Our attitudes display clearly what we think about ourselves, the people we affect and the way we feel things should be run.**
>
> **An attitude is a natural extension of a person's belief system and values.**

If a person believes it is wrong to be racist their attitude shows this. Except that it may not be too clear if other real connections are not made - like how power balances are affected between a black and white person.

This lack of clarity is even more aggravated if the white person has not tackled that old superiority problem based in hundreds of years of white colonial rule. The tin hat is then put on it if the white person does not understand that white British society relies heavily on a white belief system which actively differentiates between black and white in a most vicious and cruel methodology.

> **The belief is therefore even more powerful than the attitude .**
>
> **It now becomes a moral judgement of what is right and wrong.**
>
> **It rationalises the enforcement of power against others who are different.**

An attitude propels belief into the future and expects a course of events to follow:

> "You are of no consequence to me, so serve me quickly, politely and with goods which are of top quality."

This could also read:

> "You are not at all powerful, I am, so stop your life now and attend to my needs, make sure you respect me (because I'm so important) and I expect the resources I buy with my powerful money to be every bit the resource (source of power) it is."

The belief is one of fundamental superiority.

"I AM more important".

Cutting into beliefs which are so destructive can be done by using knowledge. Facts, figures and our own experience of what we will and won't put up with aid us in changing power balances.

There are many ways to gain personal power, this book is full of them, and so are you.

The Chapter Dealing with Violence and its Threat gives insight into different methods of dealing with other people's power when they are expecting our physical submission. The Chapter Living Assertively deals with emotional and behavioural methods.

Here are a few reminders of ways of gaining personal power:

- being assertive

- being articulate

- using intelligence

- being knowledgeable

- having ability

-        vision

-        initiative

-        stamina

-        consistency

-        charisma

- being inspiring

- speaking the minds and aspirations of others

- 'being acceptable', or knowing how to become acceptable

- providing leadership

You might add many more. These personal powers are often well ingrained in the ruling class. Schools and parents carefully groom their children in these qualities. The problem is, of course, how these powers are used.

If others of us have not been trained in managing power, how do we gain confidence to learn these skills?

Even worse, how do we develop when others are constraining us? If, as women, we have been taught not to trust in ourselves, not to have faith and especially we are told we are of little value it is no wonder we don't take opportunities to MOVE ON.

Women with disabilities are constantly hammered with anti-personal beliefs.

To believe you CAN even against the odds is a true expansion of the human spirit.

Figure 3   **Here is an outline of personal power processes:**

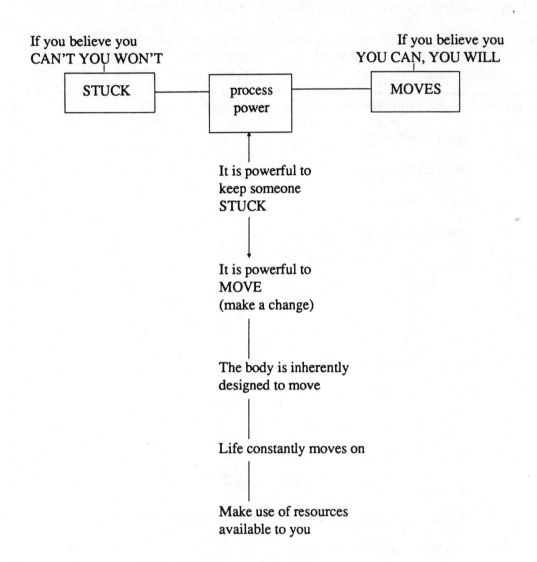

If you believe you
CAN'T YOU WON'T

STUCK

process
power

If you believe you
YOU CAN, YOU WILL

MOVES

It is powerful to
keep someone
STUCK

It is powerful to
MOVE
(make a change)

The body is inherently
designed to move

Life constantly moves on

Make use of resources
available to you

Here are further reminders of resource power:

- money
- energy
- possessions
- time
- transport
- communication / information / knowledge / words and definitions
- the ability to change the rules without sanction.

To measure the amount of power we personally have available to us:

1. Quantify how much access you have to use **resources.**

2. Consider the various areas of **your personal power.**

3. Consider the power **given to you** because ruling interests favour you.

Our personal power is then balanced with the power that other people either have or assume they have over us.

> The *integrity* of power understands our own personal capacity to affect other people and respects their needs in a spirit of equality.
>
> Our *level* of power depends on the resources available to us to influence or control people.
>
> The *capacity* of power recognises the number of people our personhood can affect and what it means to them.

Creative or Destructive Capacity

Unless we individually recognise our potential for creativity or destructiveness we will never truly acknowledge our power. This can be hard to do when it is in the ruling elite's interest to keep most of us feeling weak and of no consequence.

Destructiveness

Power can be destructive even going as far as killing.

> If you turn your energy against someone it is within your power to :
>
> **restrict them**
> **strangle them**
> **submerge them**

- It is within the power of a parent to **restrict** a child to such an extent that the child is never able to flourish and grow. As an adult they may never have the confidence to be the person they would like to be.

- It is within the power of any adult to **strangle** another - given the right circumstances and with a little bit of planning. We don't go around killing each other but we can certainly impede the personal power of another person through put-downs, criticism, negativity and defeatism.

- It is within the power of most of us to **submerge** others who may be dependent on us. We can do this by being over protective, by over indulging in resources not really needed, by taking away another person's personal power.

> Unless we realise our personal capacity for destructive power we will never properly own our true powers.

We are constantly told that we are not powerful so it seldom enters our minds that we might be destructive. And yet, we are, consistently and annoyingly so.

We are sometimes startled by our own capacity to make a mess of it all.

To understand it fully we have to go a step further. WE HAVE TO KNOW that our personal power can be and is RUTHLESS.

Confronted by the man raping your daughter you might just kill him. THAT is powerful.

Creative capacity

Our creative capacity comes also in many forms but to think of a few:

To :
> be open
> expect
> share energy
> share resources
> allow

- **To be open** to new ideas, methods, attitudes, and beliefs is to allow opportunities for yourself and others.

- **To expect** the best of and for other people is to draw out the best in them, this will probably benefit you too.

- **Sharing energy and resources allows** other people to expand and have power. It is also the basis for synergy - a phenomena where the energy of human beings combine to produce an ever growing result.

Using power creatively is the basis for producing. It is the time when we can feel useful, we are of use, something has been made.

Natural Life Cycles

Birth, living, dying can be said to be a natural life cycle.

Many occurrences can take place which may define the way we live, however. Is it natural to NOT allow any medical assistance even to the point that we might die prematurely of disease?

It is powerful to interfere with what might occur if we have means of changing natural events which may be damaging to us.

It is powerful for women to have knowledge of how their bodies function. Even more so to have aids in helping the difficult parts like menstruation and giving birth.

Finally, if the woman IS powerful she can decide what she wants to help her give birth, when and how. There aren't many women who have those privileges.

Men do control most areas of our lives, including those most intimate to us. The male gynaecologists have seen to that. We are more aware of male interference in our natural life cycles than ever before. And yet the onslaught is even greater.

We hold much personal power if we first understand how our bodies function.

Then feeling how they function in relation to what seems right to us individually.

There are no prescribed rules for what feels right to us particularly.

You are the best judge as to what is 'natural' and what is not.

It is important however, to recognise how powerfully destructive of ourselves we can be, when we rely solely on others' prescriptions of our ailments.

It is also powerfully self destructive to succumb to the pressures of this society which tells us that ageing as a woman is unattractive.

Also, that we will become useless, spent women as soon as the child bearing years are over. That is truly interference with a natural life cycle.

Reclaiming our power in that area is long overdue.

Add it to your energy and the value and knowledge you have of the resources available to you and really, we should be looking forward to an ageing population of very, very important, self respecting, wise, elderly and powerful women ....

CHAPTER 3
KNOWING OUR FEARS

In this chapter we:

Define fear

Consider what it is we are afraid of

Look at the effects of fear

Argue that oppression is a real reason to feel fear

Defining Fear

Who's afraid of the big, bad wolf?

Perhaps it depends on how big, how bad and if that wolf is likely to have any effect on me. It could be about as fearful as beauty is in the eyes of the beholder. IT after all, IS a beautiful wolf.

Fear is one of the basic human emotions which motivates us all the time. Often it lies dormantly in our sub-conscious. It is too hard to live openly with our fear - so we put it to one side, only allowing it out at dark moments. All the real terror of it then floods our system and its discomfort can be so acute that we may even be disabled by it.

> **Simply, fear is a response to a believed threat.**
> **It stimulates the whole body to behave in a defensive or offensive manner.**

A healthy fear reaction gives a person new choices because the body flows with adrenalin. This stimulates the nervous system into action, which promotes self survival.

If we understand fear and its consequences we can strive towards managing it so that we can adjust to threats in a constructive manner.

Letting fear grip our lives is to become so defensive that we will not allow anything in - which means the good as well as the bad.

Fear then controls us and stops us from taking up choices which are available to us.

Taking risks will often be fraught with anxiety and stress.

However, the key to managing fear is to question, clarify and understand the risks being taken when doing anything which appears frightening.

> **A healthy attitude to fear assumes a partnership between risk taking and analysing the threat.**

In this chapter we think about these threats and how real they are. We also think about risk-taking in a way which asks us to consider a future relationship with our fears - rather than hiding and subduing them.

What are We Afraid Of?

Fear gives us a signal. It tells us to expect that something awful may happen to us. It is an alarm and also puts us into gear for action.

Fear may result because of:

    1. Being afraid of personal damage, injury or discomfort.

    2. Being afraid of losing or not gaining something which we believe is 'ours'.

Each of us carries a history of experiences which has given us reason to be afraid.

Sometimes our personal fear is unique. Often fears will be common to many people. The fear of racism is an example of how large sections of the population share similar experiences.

Our past will often pre-determine our future reactions to circumstances.

Each of us lives with a quantity of fears which are not repeated as a pattern in other people. Usually, some fears are more dominant for us than other fears. These are highly motivating and can freeze us into immobility or motivate us to 'fight back'.

To identify what's happening for us personally we need to consider a range of threats and then analyse the ones that feel most worrying.

Analysing the Fear that Motivates Us

The first point noted above - the fear of personal damage - is a fundamental fear common to everyone save a few soul-less people convinced of their own physical might.

Damage may be anything from pure physical violence to mental damage which scores into our emotional well-being.

Injury is a further description of damage and implies some breakdown of physical or mental functioning. An injury needs to be mended if it is possible, otherwise we live with some sort of permanent damage which may have to be adjusted to. (See Chapter Becoming Able)

Discomfort can be either physical or mental also, but is not necessarily life threatening. It is uncomfortable to be restricted in one's diet by rationing, but so long as the main elements of nourishment are there we will continue to survive.

Physically, it is uncomfortable to have only a little water on tap so that we cannot have a bath each day. However, there is enough to wash in.

Emotionally, we can feel discomfort when a relationship is not going the way we want it to.

It is important to distinguish these three areas because it allows us to put a matter of degree to our analysis of what we are afraid of.

Damage, injury and discomfort can be administered in three ways:

by other people

by the elements

through ourselves.

We spend most of our lives trying to protect ourselves from the worst excesses of feeling threatened by them.

Most of the later chapters in this book give ideas and methods of minimising damage through personally learning how to cope physically.

The second point is that of being afraid of losing or not gaining something which we think is ours.

It is about what we consider to be our privileges and personal rights

---

What are our privileges?

We could say that we actually have no rights to anything, that it is all an accident of nature that we are able to take from the earth so many of its resources.

However, older cultures have consistently recognised the 'giving of the earth and sun'. The American Indian's respect and worship of the land and the sun recognises humanity using resources and living within a natural balance.

The privileges bestowed upon us in the west, by capitalism, have made us greedy. This is fermented by money-seeking opportunists who have no compunction in taking just about everything which comes their way. Unfortunately, we do get caught up in this web of gluttony and consider it also our moral right to have some of the goodies.

Behind this however, are fears of LOSING that which we are used to.

We know how awful it is to be cold and hungry - or do we?

Perhaps for some of us the actual fear is greater than the experience because we may not have ever felt EXTREME cold or hunger. **We simply have ideas about it.**

For those who have experienced such severe discomfort it can either be very motivating to NOT ever want to repeat the experience OR it can console us in the knowledge of our ability to cope under such hardship.

It is therefore important to analyse whether it is the thought of the danger which motivates us, or the reality.

Perhaps it has never entered the minds of some people that THEY might ever be hungry. They have been so well endowed by family and society that there is no question that they would ever suffer such a fate. Whereas these people cannot picture their fear or even identify it, it is they who will so often defend their privileges as if under extreme threat.

- The illogical and hostile reactions of the white people against the new black neighbours - to the extent of moving out themselves - is an example of white privilege being threatened. Their reactions are racist. But it is their fear which cannot tolerate interference in their lifestyle or economic grandeur. The irrational fear then permeates throughout the white neighbourhood, white people move out and of course the self fulfilling prophesy emerges - the value of the houses goes down.

  And all because of that first black family ......

  It is the power of racism that it breeds racism and creates fears as a mechanism to sustain itself.

To come to the bottom of our fears we have to face them and question ourselves about the difference between real life-threatening fears and the fear of losing privileges. The gifts we hold so dear to our hearts may be owned by us, but they might be whisked away from us at any time. How will we react and on *what basis* do we make decisions about whether these are privileges or not? If we assume that something is not necessarily ours (we only have its use for a period of time which could be less than we'd like) then we may cut out the FEAR OF LOSING IT.

Fear puts us into corners which can be very ugly. Especially when it is unjustified or not put into the context of a world full of equally valid people struggling for self survival.

> **We have to make difficult personal decisions about which of our privileges really are righteously ours and which are superfluous to a basic standard of living which respects the balances of life.**

What about our rights?

The fear of losing our 'rights' means a lot to us. The 'civilised' notion of rights is defined in the context of ALL individuals being free to exercise these rights.

It is more than clear however, that some people's rights are seen as more important than others. Wealth and fortune go a long way in pre-determining the level of 'rights' an individual can expect.

> **The theory suggested here is that the greater we personally consider our privileges to be 'as of right' the more likely we are to have vast fears about losing them.**
>
> **This in turn promotes a defensive reaction which can lead to violence in many forms.**

What are we afraid of losing?

It may be helpful now to look at some specific elements of living which we may be afraid of losing - and **to distinguish between what is a personal right and what is a privilege.**

The list can be as long or short as you like, but here are a few ideas:

THE FEAR OF LOSING:

shelter

food

warmth

clothing

health and exercise

other people - parents
children
relatives
friends
dependency on them

community - an identifiable group to which we belong
exchange of resources
work
group protection
self identity within group

mobility - transport
access to places you want to go to
physical movement

self - worth and self esteem
beliefs, integrity and principles
being in control
independence
movement towards personal goals
relaxation and rest
education
personal skills

Your feelings about what you think are your rights or privileges will be affected by these factors:

Your: wealth
'freedom' to make personal choices
your access and degree of use of any or all of the areas outlined
capacity to control these areas

The mix we then have is a balance between your personal power, your fear of losing your privileges and how you actually behave. However, the above list of human requirements is extremely pertinent for those who may have little or none of these resources available to them.

- Losing loved ones,
        having no personal mobility,
                losing an identity because for example,
                        society at large rejects your being a lesbian,
        these feel like the loss of important human resources.

Having lost them, or perhaps never having had them leaves us with a choice. Whether to struggle for the particular need we wish to fulfil or to leave it as a 'lost cause' or a 'finished moment'.........

The barriers we are up against in accomplishing what we want may well be restricted by other people's defensiveness or fear of losing their privileges. So, it seems important to take some personal responsibility around what we are frightened about because we may well be restricting others in their choices.

> **Understanding first what's happening in you then allows a judgement for future action which balances your needs with others' needs.**

The nine point list on page 39 merely suggests ideas for your consideration. You may wish to prioritise those which affect you the most deeply. An honest appraisal is exceedingly difficult. It is hard to distinguish between a satisfaction of superfluous need and that which is apparently basic to your survival.

Some guidelines could be simply to ask these questions:

> **If I were to lose this area of my life:**
>
> - how would I react?
> - would the circumstances of loss make a difference?
> - can I live my life without it?
> - if not, why not?

Your fears are often motivated by your past deprivation or damage.

One fear could easily dominate your whole life and everything else may be coloured by it.

The idea here is to distinguish between your survival and legitimate needs which you feel perfectly entitled to struggle for and those which are not in this category.

> **It is not a privilege to live in fear.**

Fear is a terrible burden imposed by many factors. Unravelling your personal distress is painful and sometimes terrifying, often providing a fertile bed for contradictions to surface. Fears are always uncomfortable to analyse because we subject ourselves to our facing that horrifying prospect of:

> **losing something dear to us.**

Effects of Fear

If fear is an alert system to tell us something is or may be wrong the healthy reaction to it is to do something about it.

It is commonly understood that our natural response to fear is to:

freeze

take flight

or fight

The hormone adrenalin is pumped rapidly around the body when under threat and activates everything. Mind and muscle take over and select maybe one of the above reactions. In a serious situation you may not feel at all in control. Suddenly, this 'other' person comes out and you may find yourself frozen to the ground (when you thought you'd always fight). Alternatively, you may find superhuman powers like the mother who somehow manages to lift a car off her child after an accident.

Freezing

Fear is a monumental surge of energy running through you which can electrify and warn you. The freezing action may be a way of preventing you from moving because to move may just be the wrong thing to do. Some women who have been raped have looked back and seen that their freezing actually prevented them from being killed or very badly hurt.

Flight

Taking flight is obviously an escape mechanism which in its crudest form allows you to get the hell out of there, fast!

Once again, in extreme cases this could save your life. Even when it only seems like the guy is half serious at being obnoxious, it may just be quicker, wiser and safer to go.

Fight

When afraid you may take your chances and bop the aggressor right on the nose. OK if he or she is out to do you real harm.

There are more and more accounts now of women who 'fight back' after an assault on the street. Often the indignation of being attacked mixes with fear to make a very potent explosion. The adrenalin may give the woman that extra strength to show an aggressor that SHE really means business. It has put enough men to flight for us to know it can work!

These are examples of our body using fear for what it was primarily designed to do. The hormones rushing through the blood stream are pumped into the muscles and they are instantly prepared for what comes next. A forceful action on your part will finalise the body's natural cycle. Superhuman effort will flush your system with what is expected of it.

> **Unfortunately, these days we live in such a constant turmoil of pressure that the ordinary reaction to fear is often suppressed.**

Suppressed Fear

Firstly, it is often hard to distinguish whether it is really fear we are feeling.

Secondly, the way we live often means short-cutting reactions for the sake of 'keeping things quiet' or 'not wishing to appear aggressive' or 'not wanting to seem weak'.

Thirdly, there is just too much pressure on us in this 'modern' consumerist world. We often have little real, restful time to think through what it is that is really worrying us.

Anxiety

Anxiety is closely linked to fear.

If we are anxious we are worrying about something either in the sub-conscious or overtly out there on the front line.

> **A worry is an important state of examining future actions in relation to what may happen.**

A good worry allows you to think through alternatives, anticipating problems and being afraid of the consequences. It is a futuristic attempt at reducing threats. When it's working well it's great. When it isn't it becomes a nightmare of concern which may invade sleeping patterns and produce nasty symptoms of distress.

Stress

The next chapter deals with stress and its management. Suffice it to say that stress is a result of our inability to cope with all the horrendous pressures on us.

The negative side of stress will then start to eat away at us.

> **A direct effect of fear therefore, is to experience difficult symptoms associated with being over-stressed.**

Panic

Another effect of fear is panic. It is a combination of freezing and wanting to go into immediate action. Often, action is frowned upon ie. you can't leave the classroom when you're picked on by the teacher, so you panic. Everything goes and you're left a nervous, twitching wreck unable to think of anything.

Panic is the opposite of freezing. Your reactions speed up and everything is going ten to the dozen. You can't see the wood for the trees and you feel helpless and completely out of control. Once again, this may prove to be the best way out of a situation because it is communicated to the other person and they may give up because they can see they are getting nowhere.

However, when things are going wrong and a repetition of the situation arises we may not cope with it too well. Panic starts to build on panic. Whereas our natural reaction may be to get up and leave when the boss puts on the pressure, unfortunately we're not meant to, so we stay, panic stricken.

Normally, coming up with the goods for the boss may evaporate future panics. But, if we haven't dealt with it adequately we'll be back in the old situation again, completely at the mercy of the boss.

> **This time however we are likely to feel fear about the panic AS WELL as the fear prompted by the boss.**

If this carries on we are in a vicious cycle resulting in complete immobilisation. Often there are other events in life which also combine to undermine us, specifically, depression and loss of any of the basic needs.

> **Panics are directly related to fears. Uncovering what it is that concerns us may be a difficult job but it is worth trying.**
>
> **There may be only one unpleasant memory which has aggravated our sense of loss of control.**
>
> **It is probably very valid and real. Believe it.**

It may be a comfort to know also that a repetitious panic is really a **fear of fear** and if we analyse our fears as suggested it may put more sense to it.

Phobia

A further effect of fear is to be afraid of an identifiable subject which consistently causes awful anxiety or fright. There are many forms of phobia ranging from extreme dread at the sight of a spider to complete agony at leaving the house.

The latter - agoraphobia - seems to grip women more commonly than men. The individual is unable to move freely from place to place. She may feel either panic or a sense of being completely frozen.

- Carol Anne Davis has said on living with the panic of agoraphobia in an article:-

    "At first I would simply perspire throughout the ten minute walk to the office, but within weeks my anxiety worsened and I found that I couldn't pass a bus stop in case the queue was staring at me. I began to cross roads and avoid people, and my panic grew." (1)

Carol was debilitated by her phobia. Her fear of people and space was further complicated by the recurring fear of her panics.

"I suffered increasing feelings of unreality when I was outside, as if I were somehow watching myself from above. Although I didn't know it then, this is one of the symptoms of extreme stress and fear. Finally I collapsed, hyperventilating in an attack which left me disorientated and afraid." (1)

This final collapse was enough to motivate Carol into determined effort to do something about her agoraphobia. She found therapy a help and slowly learned how to face her fears. She learnt strategies and took it very slowly asking for assistance when she needed it.

The key to Carol's management of her phobia was to acknowledge it as real. THEN she could do something about it and turn it on its head by challenging herself to confront her deep anxiety.

All of us have a sense of what a phobia is. None of us is free of fears and the less we face those fears the more they will rule us.

Sometimes a phobia can directly affect other people in very detrimental ways.

- Homophobia, the state of intense personal fear of lesbians and homosexuals, will often result in overt hostility to individuals who have not done any harm to anyone.

  The homophobe often covers up fears by diverting attention from themselves through scapegoating and bullying the lesbian or gay man.

This sort of phobia is not only offensive, it may lead to dangerous acts of persecution. In such a situation, in order for healthily balanced relationships to be secured, it is necessary for the homophobic person to uncover and confront her/his personal fears.

Perhaps this all seems extreme but, how often does fear REALLY grip us, and cause us to damage other people each day?

Obsessions

Obsessive behaviour can control an individual into performing rituals which may be repeated dozens of times in only a few hours.

- It is a compulsive behaviour, these are a few examples (2)

    - touching an object a number of times before doing anything else

    - washing hands countlessly

    - plucking hair out one strand at a time

    - spending hours checking, then re-checking, that the gas is off

    - checking there are no particles on clothes.

It is estimated that over one million people in the UK suffer from some sort of obsessiveness.

> **It is another example of 'fear gone mad' where something in the past has caused anxiety in the individual and this takes priority over everything else.**
>
> **It is important again to uncover the source of fear and to recognise that the reactions are those of fear but the obsession is a HABIT.**

Society generally, is fairly ritualistic. By definition it has to be - otherwise we'd never do the right things at the right time.

- For instance, researchers note that Catholics seem to be more likely to suffer obsessiveness and it is suggested that this is owing to the Catholic emphasis on guilt. They further note that 'a lot of obsessives are very guilt-ridden'.

  This may or may not be true, but the Catholic religion is very ritualistic. Proving yourself worthy of the faith and god's justice is a pre-dominant necessity.

  Unfortunately, this leads to fear-mongering in the shape of threatened punishments.

  The wrath of god and the gates of hell await the sinner. The overwhelming and perhaps repugnant vision of a man hanging, tortured on a tree, is enough to fill any soul with nightmares of fear and anguish.

We all understand obsessiveness. For example, superstition still prevails and can lead to seemingly irrational behaviour like 'touching wood' or throwing salt over your shoulder. Some of us subscribe more to superstition than others. It's really about 'If I don't do this something awful might happen.'

Worrying is a form of subtle obsessiveness, but it is healthy if we are not shackled to it. It is important to feel fear of terrible consequences because then we can do something to avert them.

The difference is however, whether WE FEEL IN CONTROL of our intentions and lifestyle.

Modern treatment of obsessive behaviour urges the sufferer to consider self-exposure (to the subject that frightens you) as a means of persistently attempting a self therapy. With professional guidance this may be a helpful solution. It requires the individual to face her fears and to learn about them as motivating forces in her life. The Americans have used the drug clomipramine (3) to inhibit the body's reaction and it is said to help the sufferer to say 'no' to her fear.

The use of a drug may well be the right answer for some. The biggest drawback is of course dependence on an artificial source of help. It may not feel like a personal achievement in taking back control.

Addictions

Dependency on alcohol or drugs, or dependency on any strong habit will nearly always be associated with some fear underneath it all.

> "What would happen if I didn't have alcohol available? (I might not be able to cope - with loneliness/ social relationships/ my own body/ depression/ the awful facts)."

> "What would happen if I didn't have valium? (I wouldn't be able to sleep/ relax/ cope with pressure/ live)."

Then of course the fear of withdrawal symptoms when dropping a dependency habit can be almost as frightening, if not more, than the initial fear itself. The individual is then imprisoned in a nightmare of having to manage two separate and complicated physical reactions.

It seems hard to disentangle any one chunk of life without thinking about the rest.

Analysing all the fears we have, their importance in our life and then considering our power (or energy) to overcome obstacles can start us on the right road.

> **Fear can grip every particle of our being.**
>
> **It is a tremendous source of energy.**
>
> **Re-organising that energy for your own benefit will make it work FOR you rather than against you.**

Naming the Oppressor and Oppression

Fears Are Real

It has already been noted that our fears may be truly founded on the real experience of other people wishing or threatening to damage us.

> **Fear which is associated with 'being oppressed' is often a reaction to the KNOWLEDGE that the oppressor will damage us *if we challenge their privileges.***

The knowledge may be full-frontal experience and facts of the oppressor's power. Or it may only be an insidious FEELING which still motivates us but we can't actually define. Or again, it could be pure conditioning which is completely ignorant and is subservient to the oppressor.

Which ever way you look at it, the consequence of challenging the privilege of the oppressor is to be punished - often severely and usually very swiftly.

> **Physical violence against us is an ultimate power and this obvious threat motivates us deeply. We operate from such a base of fear all the time.**

For our use here, an oppressor is defined as anyone who acts against the human rights and choices of others.

We have learnt that 'rights' are often intangible, but we hold our personal rights close to our hearts.

Sometimes we may not even realise we have certain 'rights'. Assertiveness training clearly features lists of personal rights as a means of checking oppressive (or aggressive) behaviour by others, see Chapter Living Assertively.

It is important to say that it is *easy* to oppress each other when our society is so FULL of inequalities, divisions and misunderstandings. However, it is evident that some people are more likely to oppress than others who may be more likely to become victims of oppressors.

Power Balances are Based in Fear

An oppressor is one who is prepared to win or maintain privileges at the expense of a victim. The two methods of doing this are:

1. To use;

>*a. the threat of damage against an individual*

>*b. actual force against them.*

2. To take from another person, or to deny them, resources.

1a. Threat of damage

We live constantly with the threat of male violence against us, to the extent that a lot of women will not go outside alone, at night, for fear of being attacked.

So too, the threat of racial violence in some areas of Britain is so great that many black people will not venture out alone. This is especially so in areas where the fascist British National Party is active. It may also be the case in neighbourhoods where there are fewer black people. They may be subject to clear bullying from perhaps only a handful of racists.

The fear is real and based in personal decisions about the risks of venturing out.

Some people will go out regardless of what may appear to be danger. They may have more resources available to them.

- For instance, they may have their own transport. Or they may have friends throughout the neighbourhood that they can rely on to help if there is any 'trouble'. They may be very confident because they are physically strong or emotionally experienced in dealing with threats.

There are other options in dealing with the threat of physical violence. This book outlines many. Hopefully, a woman can face her fear of racial or sexual attack, quantify how real it might be and act according to her own abilities.

Being unecessarily frightened of attack keeps many women at home, especially after dark.

1b. Actual force

Actual force is the ultimate power of the oppressor:

Taking away a woman's children.

Sacking a lesbian merely because she is a lesbian.

Incarcerating a person with a mental handicap in an institution.

Imprisoning a disproportionate number of black women for petty offences.

Riding police horses into a student demonstration.

Shooting 'rubber' bullets into crowds in Ulster.

Consistently using brute and economic force against pickets.

Rape.

Corporal punishment.

Child abuse.

Battering.

Arrests because of being black.

Racial and sexual harassment.

Stopping DSS giros.

Forcing people out of jobs.

Experimenting on people with disabilities by a public health service.

And there are always more examples

It WILL damage the victims, they WILL have reason to feel fear. The power balance lies simply in who is bigger, stronger and most ruthless in wanting to win. You will not be much match if a police horse is charging at you and you have nowhere to go. But, who is bigger and stronger is also an elusive description. The violent oppressor often only thinks in terms of violence.

It must be very, very aggravating to an oppressor to use all the force they have available and yet not succeed in MAKING THE OPPRESSED SUBSERVIENT.

The continued rebellion of the black majority in South Africa demonstrates this admirably. The human spirit is the most elusive of our resources. It is there in us all.

- Susan Griffin writes of Harriet Tubman, the black woman who gave mobility to hundreds of slaves from the Southern States to the North, through her underground railway in the 19th Century:

    "I like to think of Harriet Tubman.

    Harriet Tubman who carried a revolver,
    who had a scar on her head from a brick thrown
    by a slave master (because she
    talked back) and who
    had a ransom on her head
    of thousands of dollars and who
    was never caught, and who
    had no use for the law
    when the law was wrong." (4)

To escape actual force against you is the basic means to surviving and winning. If it is the only alternative your spirit will direct you.

- Ellen Kuzwayo (a South African black woman) knew her only alternative in surviving her husband's brutality was to leave him.

    Tragically this also meant leaving her two young children also. But, she wisely knew that 'the only way to still remain a mother (to be alive and not dead) would be to go'.

    She had to uproot and leave everything behind her. All she had was herself. She would not be dominated.

    Over her long life she has re-gathered many times and is exemplary in her belief of personal survival and a better way of living. (5)

The power balances between oppressor and opressed are FIRSTLY defined by the oppressor. Then, the oppressed has to react. She may react submissively or she might fight. She might do any number of things in between.

Unfortunately, however, it is nearly always the victim who has to do something to 'right the balance' or to recover her power.

When a victim stands up for herself and says, in effect, STOP, the oppressor will probably be quite shocked.

The oppressor will then recover from the shock - usually quite quickly - and then there will be a 'punch-back'.

> **It is suggested here that the strength of the punch-back will reflect the degree of threat of loss of privilege felt by the oppressor.**
>
> **The challenge by the oppressed demonstrates to the oppressor their own weakness and contradictions.**

2. Taking or denying resources from others

Taking resources from someone depends on the power of the oppressor to keep on taking them.

- The Welsh have had their hillsides ripped inside out by the coal industry. In the past the Welsh people have been subjected to the tyranny of English capitalists not only raiding their natural resources but also subjecting them to the humiliation of low pay and dangerous working conditions. The miners' strikes have been broken too often by the police force who have acted in the interests of the mine owners.

Taking other people's natural resources is only achieved if the victims are forcefully kept under control.

Denying resources (through prejudice for instance) still rests on the *ability ultimately* to carry it through ruthlessly.

- To deny a black woman a job because she is black is against the law. Even so, black women still complain repeatedly of 'clever discrimination' which might be hard to prove in the courtroom.

Not having the opportunity to earn money and therefore build our own personal resources will be likely to make us feel even weaker than we are and immobilise us. The power gap between ourselves and the employers will then be gigantic.

Our fear of being denied resources motivates us tremendously.

If it is important to us that our children have a sound education we may want to place them in 'good' schools. **If we have the choice** we can decide to send them to such a school, or even move to a 'better' district. The fear of our children being denied a 'good' education makes us make decisions.

> **Our having a choice gives us a lot of personal power**

Relationships

> **Some ideas for working out who is more likely to oppress another person in a relationship is to ask these questions:**
>
> * Which of you is given more authority or superiority by society?
>
> * Which of you thinks her needs are more important than those of the other?
>
> * Which of you has more resources and choices available to her?
>
> * Which of you is likely to use her power ruthlessly and in what way?
>
> * Which of you is the more afraid?

It is always best to answer these questions together if you want your relationship to thrive!

Oppressions Named - and some explanations of them

Racism is the systematic attempt to keep black people inferior and without equal resources available to them. It is perpetuated by the state in whose interests it is to keep some nations and their representatives living in Britain powerless. It is administered by individuals in a complex array of power relationships based in white supremacy.

Sexism is the systematic attempt to degrade and violate women by suggesting that they are inferior to men. It is perpetuated by the state because it is patriarchal and expects men's interests to be more valuable than women's. It is administered by individuals who believe men are entitled to exploit women for personal and economic services.

Disablism is the systematic attempt to humiliate people with disabilities through ridicule and denying physical access. It is perpetuated by the state because people with disabilities are thought to be economically unproductive and should therefore be punished. It is administered by individuals who in their superiority believe themselves to be more able.

Heterosexism is the systematic attempt to extinguish lesbians and gays from society. It is perpetuated by the state through harsh laws which suggest that lesbians and gays are less than real people. It is administered by individuals who are deeply afraid of their own sexuality and who gain privilege from heterosexuality.

Classism is the systematic attempt to maintain economic order through differences in wealth. It is perpetuated by the state through allocation of national resources into the control of only a few powerful people. It is administered by individuals who subscribe to capitalism as the answer to human organisation.

Ageism is the systematic attempt to disable those who are older through ignoring the strength, dignity and wisdom of old age. It is perpetuated by the state because it is expected that with age comes uselessness. Keeping older people unproductive allows individuals to administer ageism as a means of disregarding needs and personal power.

The list of 'isms' could and does go on. An 'ism' is a way of defining an oppression which has particular characteristics only relevant to that group of people. However, there are also some very important common elements which are similar in all oppressed groups.

> **The 'administering' of an 'ism' against another person is ALWAYS based in a superiority over the victim.**
>
> **The 'ism' is owned by the oppressor with as much ferocity as their ownership of privileges.**

It is suggested that we make personal decisions all the time about other people, their strengths and weaknesses in relation to our own. We may not analyse it but our attitudes are displayed as clearly as the amount of hair we have on our bodies.

Often our attitudes are fuelled by ignorance and hearsay.

We are the administers of 'isms' and unfortunately, the fact that we are oppressed in one way DOES NOT NECESSARILY stop us from feeling superior over other groups.

Indeed, it is the intention of the ruling classes to keep people separated from each other through prejudice.

It is perfectly natural to feel fear of another person's superiority because there is an *intention* to subjugate you in some way. It is done through your feeling humiliated and worthless.

Other common components of 'isms' are the methods used against the oppressed. Being made invisible - as if you are not there - is all part of keeping you small and powerless. You're not expected to get any of the goodies, if you're not there. Being dismissed as if you are powerless is also a characteristic the oppressor will use. Fear of these rather awful behaviours against us will often subdue us and keep us 'in our place'.

> **BUT:**
>
> **FEAR IS VITAL**

Acknowledging your fears is the first step to understanding your own personal power.

During a conversation with the author, Veena, an Asian woman (whose philosophy of life has been informed by her Hindu religion, her years of living in Africa and her present lifestyle in Britain), had these comments to make:

'If you are true to yourself you will be fearless. Not only knowing your fear but being true to yourself about the fear and about all things complex and simple. If we are aware that someone else is lying we need to keep calm and next time we are more cautious. They will sense or see our caution and then the other individual can often become more fearful themselves. This can give us power. I want to eliminate fear so that there is that mutual trust which will promote understanding. That has to be built gradually and is dependent on both parties.' (6)

Accepting that the danger is REAL allows you then to organise yourself around it.

It provides a healthy stress factor which gives you an opportunity to use to your benefit.

You can:

> take back control
>
> > fight
> >
> > > take flight

Fear is a motivator:

> It can help you:
>
> > to get up and go
> >
> > > get up and succeed

It can WAKE YOU UP!

Recommended Reading

Feel The Fear And Do It Anyway
Susan Jeffers   Century Hutchinson   1987

Beyond Fear
Dorothy Rowe   Fontana   1987

Living With Fear
Isaac Marks   McGraw Hill   1989

The Boy Who Couldn't Stop Washing
The experience and treatment of obsessive-compulsive disorder.
Judith Rapoport   Collins   1990

Obsessive Thoughts And Behaviour
Help for obsessive-compulsive disorder.
Frederick Toates   Thorsons   1990

Agoraphobia
Ruth Hurst Vose   Faber & Faber   1981

Who's Afraid Of Agoraphobia?
Facing up to fear and anxiety a self-help guide.
Alice Neville   Century Arrow   1986

Women And Tranquillisers
Celia Haddon   Sheldon Press   1984

The Tranquilliser Trap And How To Get Out Of It
Joy Melville   Fontana   1984

Compulsion
Jealousy, alcoholism, eating, drugs, work, sex.
Robin Blake and Eleanor Stephens   Boxtree   1987

Call Me Woman
Ellen Kuzwayo   Womens Press   1988

Organisations:

The Phobics Society   4 Cheltenham Rd, Manchester M21 1QN

The Open Door Association (for agoraphobic people) 447 Pensby Rd, Haswall, Merseyside

The Phobic Trust 51 Northwood Ave, Purley, Surrey

Women And Alcohol Camberwell Council on Alcoholism, Tavistock 1980.

Alcoholics Anonymous 11 Redcliffe Gdns. London SW10 Tel 071 352 9779

Alcohol Concern 305 Grays Inn Rd, London WC1X 8QF Tel 071 833 3471

Action On Smoking And Health 5 - 11 Mortimer St, London W1   Tel 071 637 9843

Drugs, Alcohol And Women Nationally
349 North Rd, London N7 9DP Tel 071 700 4653

Tranx 52a Masons Ave, Wealdstone, Harrow , Middlesex HA3 5AH Tel 081 427 2827

CHAPTER 4
MANAGING STRESS

In this chapter we look at:

Re-defining stress

    Symptoms

        Causes

            Cycles

                Breaking Out

                    Methods of Breaking out

Stress Re-defined

'Stress' is a much maligned word.

Unfortunately we have extraordinary connotations of it. They are probably dominated by an image of a highly paid white male executive who is a workaholic and about to have a heart attack.

The vistas have broadened considerably over the last few years however, as the wider population realises its susceptibility to the destructive side of stress.

Even so, that male vision of not being able to cope under extreme pressure still lingers on. Having too much to do in too little time means that achievement is at a premium. The male notion of stress is too often linked with the need for success and individual primacy. The nasty symptoms of 'stress' seem to stop the man from going further. He is, after all, a human being!

'Stress' has been put on the national agenda because of two significant factors:

1.   The workforce ARE being affected by 'cut and thrust' policies of ruthless production orientation - they can't keep up.

2.   The population is horribly unhealthy as we began to realise when we learned that Britain was top of the league for Heart Disease - nearly one third of the population under 75 die from coronary heart disease, and another third from cancer. (7)

Both of the above have forced a dreadful public acknowledgement that people are dying through combinations of 'stress', diet, alcohol and smoking. A male reaction pre-dominates. It is no coincidence that the NHS is top heavy in equipment and surgery related to male illness like heart attacks. These are the 'productive people' in society, so they have to be protected and looked after.

If we put all this to one side and look at a more analytic description of what is actually happening to women when WE don't cope the picture is a little clearer.

> **When it's not going right, or we're not coping or we're being swamped by circumstances we feel**
>
> *DISTRESS.*

WE are able, because of sexist conditioning, to accept the feelings we have and to describe them in an accurate way.

DISstress suggests a malfunction of some sort.

It actually OWNS what is happening to the body and because of that allows us an opportunity to do something about it - usually STOP. It is distressing to be in pain. We have to stop to cry or talk it over with a friend or feel miserable.

Stress, technically, describes the action of the body against a stimulus. The body will not move unless we put stress on certain muscles to move it (see Chapter Knowing our Bodies)

> **Stress is a normal and healthy response to LIVING and also of succeeding to live. Men have taken over this word because they find it impossible to accept that they are malfunctioning when suffering symptoms of OVER stress. The result of over-stress is distress.**

It is even more worrying to the male ego to accept failure so masking it by using a positive word like stress lets them half off the hook. The stress explanation does not, by definition however, ask the individual to consider analytically what it is that is *causing distress*.

Think about how much fear stimulates distress and the male inability to face their fear. For men to acknowledge fear and own it is for them also to realise their infallibility - to be less than they thought of themselves.

Have you also fallen into the trap of not being able to face fear?

For the purposes of this book then, STRESS is seen as a positive life-giving stimulation to parts or all of our bodies.

> **Stress strengthens us through experience, learning and development of our physique and mental attributes. It gives us power because we have challenges in our life and we look to them to be overcome and enjoyed.**

Under-stress occurs when an individual suffers too little stimulation.

Over-stress is the condition of having too much stimulation. Some people can cope with over-stress and even seem to thrive on it.

It only appears OVER the top because most of us couldn't handle that much. If there really is TOO much for us to *cope* with THEN we start to feel distress. The result of this is that we experience any or all of the major symptoms we are beginning to know so much about.

> **They ARE indicators of a creature in DISTRESS.**

They are not flattering and they can make us feel inadequate and even immature when we realise how much our lives are being dominated by such strength of reactions. It is useful always to examine first our symptoms of distress.

Most distress will have some strong elements of fear in it. Our body reactions when distressed will therefore be as described in the last chapter. The following is merely a list of some of the more obvious symptoms of distress that we can feel. There are many more, and you are likely to know of them. For our purposes, we shall just examine a few.

Symptoms of Distress

There are four main headings under which symptoms may be categorised.

The central feature of *loss* suggests that this is the most significant aspect to our feelings of distress.

> 1   Loss of self worth.
>
> 2   Loss of control.
>
> 3   Loss of healthy body reactions.
>
> 4   Loss of the ability to relax.

By looking at the symptom under one or more of these headings we are led inevitably to ask the question WHY are we experiencing such a reaction?

It is the first step in acknowledging our distress.

Here are some examples of symptoms under each heading:

1   Loss of Self Worth

* Low self esteem   * Can't get up in the morning

* Nervousness   * Withdrawal and daydreaming

* Depression   * Excessive concern about health

* Lack of confidence   * Feel like you have no friends

* Unable to find personal support

2   Loss of Control

* Compulsive behaviour ie: Over or under eating
                              Alcohol dependency

* Anger at trivia   * Inappropriate impatience

* Confusion   * Unable to prioritise

* Hyper-activity   * Excitability

* Difficulty in completing tasks

* Nervous breakdown

* Weepiness

* Demotivation

* Irritability

* Lack of concentration

* Grief

* Boredom

* Accident - proneness

* Absenteeism from work

3   Loss of Healthy Body Reactions

* Headaches

* Unaccountable pains
   (often termed psychosomatic)

* Palpitations

* High blood pressure

* Angina

* Stroke

* Indigestion

* Ulcers

* Diarrhoea or constipation

* Asthma

* Tension in muscles causing pain

* Backache

* Stiffness in shoulders and neck

* Menstrual irregularities

* Skin rashes

* Tingling in arms or legs

* Double vision

4   Loss of Ability to Relax

* Unable to sleep properly

* Waking up too early

* Not able to settle to any one activity

* Not easy to find other people to
   relax with

* Can't find energy to enjoy a hobby

* Can't stay still

Feeling distress CAN make us feel like a 'loser'. Perhaps we need to think what it is we have lost though. The above four categories illustrate how easy it is to lose bits of ourselves in the rush to live in the 1990's.

It is always beneficial therefore to *separate* out the *symptom* of distress from the actual *cause* of distress.

It might be useful to draw up your own list of distress symptoms, personal to you. It may be advantageous to keep the four headings and to see if there are any patterns.

MY PERSONAL LIST OF DISTRESS SYMPTOMS

First   Write down all the reactions you know you have when you are distressed.

       REMEMBER, this INCLUDES the times when you have had a 'good cry', been anxious about the safety of the people you love and felt inferior or threatened.

Second Check it for accuracy and honesty.

Third   If it brings up any distress in you take a break!

Fourth Separate out the symptoms under the four headings on a new sheet of paper.

       I feel: Loss of self worth
                   Loss of control
                   Loss of healthy body reactions
                   Loss of ability to relax

Fifth   Take a look to see if the clusters give you any indication as to deep seated causes of distress. Look also at whether your behaviour patterns have been life-long or whether they are more recent.

Later on in this chapter we examine methods of breaking out of the symptoms of distress.

Causes of Distress

Your causes of distress will be as unique to you as your past history is. Some people flourish on stress, others find the same conditions distressing.

There are many reasons for us to feel distress in our lives:

   * Feeling or having lack of power

   * Being afraid - because of all the reasons listed in the last chapter

   * Symptoms of distress further generating 'not being able to cope'

   * Assuming ourselves not to have choices

   * Not being in control

Added to these overall dimensions are three more important factors which particularly tend to cause women distress:

1. Women are more likely to be in the position of caring for other people - therefore their worries become ours too.

2. Women are economically less able to purchase 'ways out' of distress than are their male counterparts.

3. Women, in our diversity, have many different oppressive constraints in our lives which are actively constructed to undermine our attempts at being powerful or in control.

So, try matching up your list of symptoms with these questions:

1.   How much do the people I care for, or who are dependent on me, interfere with my personal needs and aspirations?

2.   How much could I change a cause of distress if I had the resources to do something about it? THINK BIG!

3.   What are the different forms of oppression I live with which affect my sense of self worth, ability to succeed and be in control?

Not Being in Control

Control is an unpopular word because it too often gets mixed up with controlling and the ensuing sense of being controlled.

To be in control is just about basic to all forms of productive, efficient and creative human activity. Not much gets done very well if participants are not in control. Or, rather it may get done, but at the expense of some individuals being exploited or abused.

When we are not in control we feel unable to do many important and self protective things:

We may not feel able to:

*   think clearly

*   work out what we want

*   make decisions

*   own our future

If you suffer from any or all of these characteristics you will probably be feeling pretty helpless.

GAINING BACK CONTROL

is something you are as entitled to do

as breathing the air.

- A black woman in one of my training sessions, fed up with the white racism around her, explained how she assumes her right to be in control. "I walk in the room AS IF I OWN IT", she said.

That is usually only reserved for the ruling classes.

Being in Control

If we are personally in control we may be said NOT to be overcome by distress.

WE ARE ABLE to get on with our life productively.

If an individual is in control she:

1st: Brings back a sense of self worth.

2nd: Brings back an understanding of what she can do and can't do in life.

This will be understood in relation to using her privileges or to her lack of them.

3rd: Lives constructively with her fears in terms of the risks she is prepared to take.

4th: Allows herself to feel the power she has and be powerful.

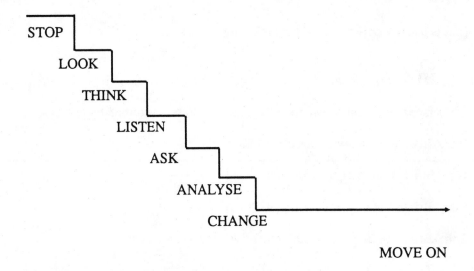

Stopping helps us to stay still for a while and really give ourselves a chance to see the wood for the trees. Do it at the first possible moment best suited to you.

Looking at the problems in the way already outlined in this chapter allows you to *think*.

Listening to yourself first and then to others second, keeps you in touch with inner feelings and other feedback.

Asking other people how they see it may give you valuable information and insight into how to tackle the problems.

Analysing the situation in a new light may open up possiblities you had never dreamt of before - if you let yourself.

Changing stops the cause of distress and can only be the right thing to do if you know that the distress will make you ill.

It's what we do when we want to cross a busy road. We have concern for our
future actions in relation to the obvious danger ahead.

Life IS dangerous.

STOP   LOOK   AND   LISTEN!

The Cycles of Stress

We have noted that 'stress' in its purest, technical form, is a description of what happens when the body reacts to an external stimulation.

We put stress on the body when we use muscles to lift food to our mouth. It is a combination of your body moving the food and the effect that the movement has on your body - BECAUSE of the food.

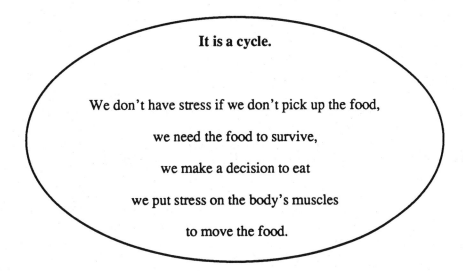

It is a cycle.

We don't have stress if we don't pick up the food,

we need the food to survive,

we make a decision to eat

we put stress on the body's muscles

to move the food.

Everything is fine if the food is nutritious, already prepared and appetising. There appears to be little stress exerted if we are relaxed and all we have to do is 'shovel it in'. It is even enjoyable. But, food (the external stimulus) is not always like that.

If you have little or no movement in your arms, the effort to raise the fork to the mouth could be enormous. Indeed, that effort, coupled with public humiliation if eating in a hostile environment, could prove to be so 'stressful' that you might go hungry instead. Your reaction to the stimulus - food - could well be one of distress.

Consider again all the distress associated with not having enough food, the anxiety and hurt involved in not being able to eat as much as you know you need. Or, the preparation of food could also be so fraught that eating it could provoke a sense of agony or misery.

We bounce along from one stimulation to the next. Often, we get locked into habits which we have fallen into for some good reason way back in the past, but still engage in because 'that's just the way I've always done it.' Unfortunately, 'Bad Habits' somehow seem to get 'worse'.

> **The question is: is it the external stimulus which is the problem, or is it you?**

Is it really, the cream cake or is it you?

Is it really, 'naughty but nice' or is it what the manufacturers have pumped and primed us to respond to?

Is it the cake or is it all those old habits and needs flooding in compelling you to eat, BECAUSE THERE IS NO OTHER ALTERNATIVE?

Or do you just like it and don't care?

> **We are living in a society which bombards us, especially as women, with** instructions,
> commands,
> demands,
> imploring,
> beseeching
> and conditioning.

We keep getting cornered by all these expectations and they press us into responding. They add frills and fancies to what is usually just a common, basic experience. The cake.

All this external pressure on us, purely because we are women adds horrendous stress to what might have been ordinary.

> **We end up having to react to other people's expectations of us nearly all the time.**

When we do respond to such overbearing pressure we often find ourselves 'locked in' to distress as a natural reaction to what is actually a horrible way to have to live. Too often, we cope with our own distress as well as all the heavy external demands, and carry on trying to function.

We get caught in a cycle of stress from an external stimulus and our reaction to it.

If we are coping and in control we will react strongly and decisively. If we are not coping well, we will start to feel distress and the loss of control and all those other symptoms already described.

Breaking Out

One way to break-out of a cycle of stress is to STOP letting that external stimulus get to us.

The other way is to change the EFFECT the stimulus has on us.

> **There is a balance here between:**
>
> - Our available choices to STOP the cause of stress
>
> - Our being FORCED to react to the cause of stress.

Stopping the Cause of Stress

If we are able to make a choice and stop the cause of our distress we have a healthy reaction to a stimulus which we believe to be negative in our lives.

We can break-out of a cycle of stress because we are in control and feeling strong.

Being Forced to React to the Cause of Stress

It has been argued that the external stimulus is merely something outside ourselves which WE react to. We might react to it positively or negatively.

If we have a difficult or distressing reaction and are forced still to be involved with the stress, then we have to manage its effect upon us.

Being in an over-stressed job

Being an over-stressed parent

Having a boring and repetitious occupation

Being harassed

Having too many things to do all at once

Having ill-health

Living with uncertainty

Having no money

These are all reasons for not being able easily to change the circumstances you are in.

- The boss is tearing hell out of you. You cannot leave your job at present for sound economic and practical reasons. Somehow you have to live with this abusive power relationship at least until your child starts school.

Once you have examined the symptoms of distress which the boss provokes in you, you can allow yourself to find other responses.

> **STOPPING to consider the effects gives you a reason to explore new behaviour patterns.**

If you are always one to panic as soon as the boss enters the room, perhaps you can learn another way to respond which maintains your control. If you withdraw and allow the boss to bully you, perhaps some assertiveness training could help.

Methods of Breaking-out

The diagram on page 66 displays two responses to an external stimulus:

1. Our positive response to stress - which is healthy and beneficial to us.

2. Our negative response - which is unhealthy and distressing.

Figure 4

The Cycles of Stress

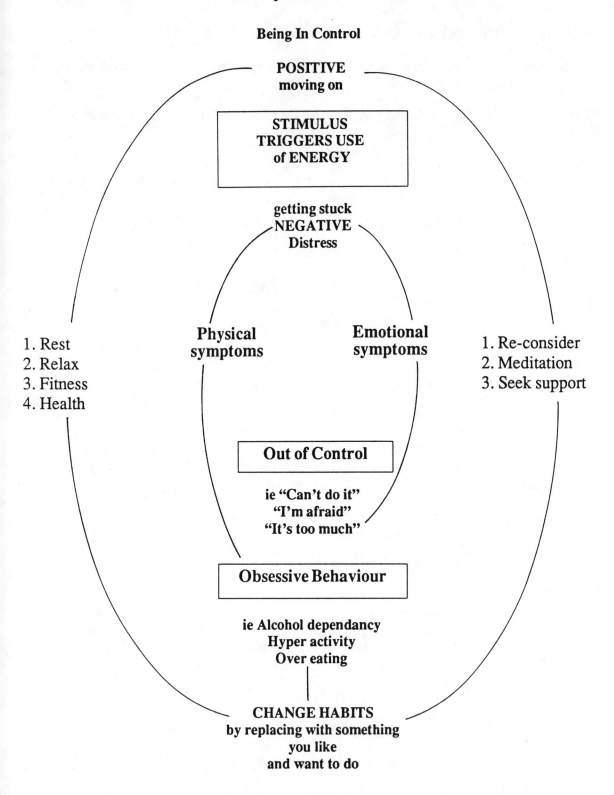

Being In Control

POSITIVE
moving on

STIMULUS
TRIGGERS USE
of ENERGY

getting stuck
NEGATIVE
Distress

Physical
symptoms

Emotional
symptoms

1. Rest
2. Relax
3. Fitness
4. Health

1. Re-consider
2. Meditation
3. Seek support

Out of Control

ie "Can't do it"
"I'm afraid"
"It's too much"

Obsessive Behaviour

ie Alcohol dependancy
Hyper activity
Over eating

CHANGE HABITS
by replacing with something
you like
and want to do

Changing the NATURE or the EFFECT of the stimulus can help you 'BREAK OUT'

The purpose now is to examine different ways of getting into the 'positive mode'. Sometimes, just trying one method can open up a completely new experience. Perhaps that one may not be suitable, but another may be.

Here are some ideas:

Re-considering

Seeking support

Meditation

Rest

Relaxation

Time management

Fitness

Health

The rest of this book!

Re-considering

Behind all the stopping, looking and analysing is one, basic, human desire.

You must WANT to re-consider.

No number of bulldozers, policemen or psychotherapists are going to get you to analyse and think about anything if you don't want to. There is no point in giving yourself hope if you don't give yourself the WILL to open up possibilities of discovering insight into yourself. Some of it will be painful. Some of it will be logically reassuring.

We cannot underestimate the toil of self discovery, but we can't move on usually unless we've done some self appraisal. If you don't want to re-consider you have at least made a personal decision to remain closed. That in itself may be helpful, but often, it will only give temporary assistance.

Seeking Support

Some people like to think alone. Some people find help in being given support by others to assist them through the painful patches of re-appraisal. When we are in a deeply troubling state of mind help from other people can be like an oasis.

Help from other people is a privilege and choice which may be far more available to some than others.

If we are lonely or isolated this may seem like a sour and out-of-date fruit, succulent for others, completely unacceptable to us.

The essential core to seeking support is to find some sort of **nourishing contact with other people.** The range is actually enormous:

Personal contact - such as that with friends, partners, relatives or close work colleagues.

Professional contact - with medical practitioners, through the National Health Service or alternative medicine. This may be specialist help in either physical or emotional needs or both.

Relaxation contact - through pursuit of leisure activities and hobbies.

Learning contact - by engaging in a course of education either at home or at an establishment.

Work contact - so long as it is productive and not a cause of distress!

Religious or spiritual contact - through your chosen religion or belief.

Reading contact - which reassures your thinking and illustrates that other humans also feel the same way.

Listening contact - by using the telephone, radio or music equipment.

Visual contact - by watching the TV or people engaged in activity you find reassuring (this could be as little as watching people walk down the street you live on) or going to spectate at an activity.

Campaigning contact - which provides a forum to 'fight a cause' either political or charity.

Adventurous contact - through travelling and exploring the way different people live.

Common interest contact - which brings people with the same interests together.

The important elements to all this contact, where seeking support is concerned are:

Feeling nourished

Experiencing some recognition of a common human emotion or activity

Finding some sort of reassurance

A luxurious aspect of seeking support will be to find beneficial guidance through a difficult period. This may not come from the supportive person or people. It could come from your analysis. So, for instance, watching women on TV achieve could prompt you to 'move on' and have a go at it yourself.

The key to all this is that when we are desperate we often feel completely bogged down by our circumstances. We do not necessarily have to pay for professional help to guide us through.

If we just allow ourselves to realise how important human contact is, and how we rely on it, we may broaden our alternative means of finding it.

Meditation

Meditation goes beyond 'having a good think'. It is really quite different.

> **Meditation is a particular state of mind which brings together the functioning of the whole body.**

It also elevates us into our surroundings *as if we are part of them*. This could be our immediate personal space, or it could be as far away as a prayer for a friend in a foreign land.

Meditation is not confined to the yogi or guru. It is an ordinary part of life which we all engage in but in varying degrees. Meditation helps. It brings us back to our core in relation to our chosen perception of our environment. It is not escapism. It is a cooperation between you, a living being, and that which affects you.

It is an acceptance of where you're at.

Here are some examples of different forms of meditation:

Thorough absorption in a simple activity:

This is the reason why basket weaving is traditionally given as a therapeutic method of 'rehabilitating' those who are mentally distressed.

Knitting is another pastime which relies on repetitive activity. However, the combination of 'doing something' with absorption allows for a meditative state and hours can pass without having actively thought of very much at all.

The important point about this however, is that the activity provides *some* stimulation to the body, minimal as it is. There is still therefore a reason to exist, a purpose to be fulfilled, a satisfaction in finishing.

The reason that people actually do survive factory work is because they can go into 'meditative mode' and repeat simple motion all day.

Distress arises more often through poor, hazardous or downright dangerous working conditions. This will accentuate a sense of boredom because the body is uncomfortable or the individual is afraid.

Having thorough involvement in your personal environment:

Sitting, standing, walking or any activity which is methodical, familiar and SAFE can allow for a meditative state.

The important factor is to want to be doing NOTHING ELSE, at that time. There is an absorption of the environment which features in this.

Prayer:

Is not only owned by the christian church. It has been taken from us by religion as a useful means of meditative *communication*.

The essence of prayer is that of having faith. It is a personal attitude of 'giving over' to something far greater than ourselves and which we may not understand. It gives a sense of allowing rather than controlling.

Prayer assumes our insignificance in the universe.

It brings us back to nothing in order to become open for eventualities over which we have no control. It can be a safety valve. Unfortunately, christianity has introduced dependency on its bureacracy to increase the sense of worshippers 'not being in control' of their own lives. That has distorted and nearly served to destroy the REAL power of prayer.

Through prayer we can tune into other people and events without understanding them. We allow ourselves to be helpless because we ARE helpless. Sometimes this can draw us into acknowledging that the only best course is to follow our feelings rather than try to analyse them.

Forms of prayer are not just clasping hands together, though this can energise the body. Staring at a candle while thinking hopefully about one single thing can have the same effect.

Pure Meditation:

In its purest form, meditation relies on complete silence and stillness, physical comfort, flow of body energy and thoroughly immersing oneself into the depths of the mind. It is a very deep form of relaxation and renewal.

> **It can be achieved through repetition of a very simple word or the constant examining of a shape or object. It is an ancient behaviour which has sustained humanity through many tribulations.**

Any or all of these three alternatives may give opportunities to 'break-out' from a destructive cycle of distress. Many of us rely on a lot of these already. However, it may be worth re-kindling old activities or starting new ones. These are areas which attend to the emotional side of stress.

On the physical side, rest, relaxation, time management, fitness and health will all contribute to our sense of being in control.

Rest

We all need different amounts but every human needs some. Rest basically is good old-fashioned sleep. Easy for some, torture for others. We sleep 'easy' when we are safe, warm, uninterrupted and nothing is troubling us. For those of us who have difficulties we need to try a variety of approaches to our sleeping routine. Identifying a cause for not sleeping well is the first step to doing something about the problem. Sometimes there is no alternative.

A crying baby HAS to be attended to and you also HAVE to earn a living. At least knowing that you are being disabled by your circumstances allows you to feel tired without guilt. It will also put reason to your other distress signals.

The hope for this situation is that children eventually stop crying at night. If you have a long-term sleeplessness problem perhaps something has to give, or rather change and maybe a long-term goal for you to work towards will help.

> **Rest is known to keep us functioning at the right levels.**
>
> **After exertion our bodies need to replenish energy, synthesise food, heal, renew old tissue and develop.**

All living creatures have dormancy periods. When we are over-stressed it is difficult to rest because so much needs to be done. We do have to make a conscious decision under these circumstances to allow ourselves rest.

> **Sleep is not the only form of rest.**

Rest is really 'taking a break' (from our cycle of stress) and stopping activity. The body will respond by lowering the blood pressure, breathing may become slower, muscles relax and the mind empties.

Relaxation

The best method of inducing rest is to engage in relaxation. It is important to remind ourselves what relaxation is.

> **Relaxation is a means of obtaining a restful state in the body. The inevitable outcome of relaxation (as any good relaxation teacher knows) is that we will go to sleep if we are tired and thoroughly relaxed.**

To relax implies that we do something to get to rest. We know there are many methods of relaxing and lots of them coincide with many of the categories outlined in Seeking Support and Meditation.

Often, if we are enjoying an activity we can be quite relaxed about it, even if we are very busy and highly stimulated. It is the transition from the busy-ness to rest which relaxation fosters. We CAN'T be busy all the time.

There are therefore, methods to help the process which have become popular over the last decade. They rely on an understanding of the body and the way it works. The basis is always dependent on the muscles of the body relaxing.

The Chapter Protect Your Back and Lift It describes the major muscle groups. It's a good idea to know where they are because when you strain one you'll know what it is and what it does for you.

Relaxation through breathing:

We can induce relaxation through a controlled and regular breathing. This can be done by counting a repeated number on exhaling as well as inhaling.

We can also bring our breathing back to a more normal rhythm from a state of hyper-ventilation (over breathing - therefore taking in too much oxygen) by slowing and deepening our breath. Or from too little breathing where we can nearly stop inhaling - the answer then is to exhale deeply because the natural response of the lung muscle is to pull in air.

Concentration on the muscles used in breathing is also a technique used to become relaxed. Imagine the air entering the nostrils, moving down the wind pipe into the lungs and filling them. Then pushing the air out from the waist up through the rib cage and up the wind pipe to be expelled out of the mouth is another calming method.

Visualising your breathing pattern to be that of the sea lapping against the shore or using music to find a sense of easy breathing rhythm can also be useful.

Relaxation through conscious muscle use:

Tension release methods ask you systematically to go through your body first tensing muscles and then relaxing them. It is a useful way of discovering tension areas.

The Alexander Technique is based in understanding your posture and identifying how not to mis-use your body. It is an excellent means of learning how you use your body in relation to stress.

The Mitchell Technique accurately suggests that muscles are best able to relax by exerting tension in the opposite direction to the muscles which are tensed. This exertion then induces relaxation.

Yoga is an exercise which stretches muscles as compliments to each other. It is a very thorough and self conscious means of tensing and relaxing through exerting pressure on the major muscle groups, often by using your own body weight and natural extension.

Massage - especially that which is thorough and is knowledgeable of muscle groupings - will deeply penetrate into muscle fibres and loosen them.

Deep heat treatment merely warms tissues thus allowing further mobility. Saunas do this by heating up the body so much that muscles HAVE to relax - especially if you are lying down.

Relaxation through other methods:

All relaxation techniques depend on muscles relaxing. Some are not quite as obvious as those above.

Visualisation - allows your imagination to take you to a place where you have been relaxed in the past, as does guided fantasy work. Your recollection reassures you and tension will drop from your muscles.

Music - once again, a sense of safety, rhythm and reassurance will provide a reaction for your body to relax.

Acupressure, reflexology, aromatherapy - are all examples of methods which rely on the body conveying messages and stimulus to other points which are in need of balancing.

They can be very effective means of releasing and using innate body energies and self regulating mechanisms.

Your own methods, favoured and consistent give you a personal sense of individuality and sometimes secret enjoyment. Remember and treasure them. Time-tested and true they provide you with a deep sense of security in yourself.

Find the time to allow yourself to become part of your favourite activity. If, for some reason, it has become impossible to do what you really like, look for new ways of re-discovering those familiar feelings.

> **They're yours and they're precious.**

Time Management

> **Managing your time is all about:**
>
> * How you want to use your time
>
> * What activities you HAVE to do
>
> * What other people's demands on you are

Part of reducing distress will be to re-allocate time so that you are more in control of it and more able to make decisions around what you want to do.

> Start by analysing how you have used your time in the past.
>
> Examine how you are using it now.
>
> How do you want to use your time in the future?

> **TIME IS EVERYTHING WE DO**

Fitness

To be 'fit' is something, supposedly, we all want to be. Sometimes, we have a few illusions of grandeur about it and are shocked to find how 'unfit' we are when the kids want us to race them.

We have a perception of fitness often left over from school days when we may have been running around a lot more then. We were also probably subjected to some measurements of how fit we were through competition.

Unfortunately, unsympathetic teaching methods in Physical Education have often left many girls feeling unhappily disgusted. So, we take with us into adulthood a whole suitcase of baggage full of lingering experiences.

LET'S GET OVER THE SCHOOL EXPERIENCES FIRST:

1. Fitness is something that has to be sustained by you. As an adult you have no teacher telling you (badly) that you must go onto the hockey field, period and all.

    What you may have is a wagging finger in the brain which has replaced her.

    YOU have to decide to be fit, in relation to what you feel your own abilities are. Find new ways of doing it. Read, ask, look for others who may feel the same way, try out new experiences, find out about your body.

2. See if you can find a teacher to help at a Sports Centre or Adult Education class. She/he may give you back faith in good teaching methods. Be aware that if the teacher replicates any of the 'nasty stuff' you had as a child that it will make you feel child-like. Perhaps it would be better to do another class.

3. Competition is overtly used to put people down and make some feel inferior. This is not a particularly helpful means of getting people to learn enjoyably. Competition leaves some at the bottom of the pile for the glory of others. This is wholly unforgivable and is not what 'good sport' is about.

    There is a growing movement in the UK which actively rejects a competitive base for fitness and sport. Many good women coaches know that they will not in any way want to induce feelings of inferiority in their participants.

    Find leaders who subscribe to this if competition has ever troubled you.

    Don't let the ultra-fashionable aerobics teacher (or your fellow exercisers) put you off. IF it still seems like the class is too competitive and it is damaging - SAY SO!

4. Measuring how 'good you were' came in the teaching package at school. It was too often done in relation to other girls' ability.

    The only measurement where our own fitness is concerned should be about how fit WE are.

    WE take responsibility for our own bodies and find ways of measuring our fitness. A lot of gyms have methods to help you do this now. If one is not available for you there are many books which can help you to do it for yourself.

THESE ARE THE COMPONENTS OF FITNESS THAT YOU WILL WANT TO MEASURE:

Your heart:
> Its resting and activity beating levels.

Your stamina:
> How long you can keep your heart beating fast when you're exercising hard.

Your muscles:
> How strong they are.

Your endurance:
> How long you can keep your muscles moving when you make them work.

Your flexibility:
> How far a muscle can stretch to move your arm or leg or any other part of your body.

Your speed:
> How quickly you can do it!

Your coordination:
> How your body works as a whole, whether it's together as a unit or disorganised.

So, throw out the rubbish in your nice suitcase brought with you from school and fill it up with that expansive attitude which is you wanting to take control of your own fitness.

There are many methods of 'keeping fit'. Understanding your fitness as outlined above challenges you to consider your whole body and its needs. Different sports will give you different benefits. So for instance, weight training helps your muscles strengthen while yoga helps you stretch them. Running gives you good exercise for the heart while T'ai Chi Chuan coordinates the whole body.

The good all round exercises, which give you multiple benefits are:

Gardening	Aerobics	Swimming	Rowing
	Dancing	Gymnastics	Judo

Health

The easily said word but the hard-to-maintain state.

Health is a physical and mental organisation of well being.

We hardly ever reach full 'health' in this obsessive and polluted society.

Distress is a major factor in ill-health and can be induced as we know, by many variables. Understanding preventative health care reaffirms our personal knowledge of ourselves and our needs.

Doing something about keeping healthy or becoming as healthy as we are able to be constantly gives us oppportunities of 'moving on.' The following chapters give practical information on how to keep healthy in a multitude of ways. They also provide a backdrop from which to approach life. You can be a whole woman anticipating challenges and struggles with knowledge of what's good for your own health and methods to achieve it.

Gaining back control from destructive stress allows us to use our bodies and safeguard our health.

As the song goes, 'It's never too late ... to change your mind'.

In which case you may be changing old habits which are not helpful to you.

BREAK-OUT!

Recommended Reading

Your Complete Stress Proofing Programme
Leon Chaitow   Thorsons   1983

Stress And Relaxation
Jane Madders   Martin Dunitz   1979

Relaxation
Modern techniques for stress management
Sandra Horn   Thorsons   1986

Simple Relaxation
Laura Mitchell   Murray   1977

Relaxation And Meditation Techniques
L. Chaitow   Thorsons   1983

The Bond Of Power
Meditation and wholeness
J. Pearce   Routledge and Kegan Paul   1981

T'ai Chi Chuan - The Technique Of Power
Horwitz, Tem et al.   Rider   1979

The Alexander Principle
Wilfred Barlow   Arrow Books   1985

Yoga For The Disabled
Howard Kent   Thorsons   1985

Yoga For You
I. Devi   Thorsons   1972

Motherwit - A Feminist Guide To Psychic Development
(Exercises for Healing, Growth and Spiritual Awareness)
Diane Mariechild   Crossing Press   1981

Everybody's Guide To Nature Cure
H.Benjamin   Thorsons   1977

Everybody's Guide To Homeopathic Medicines
Cummings S & D Ullman   Gollancz   1986

Aromatherapy For Women
Maggie Tisserand   Thorsons   1985

Human Potential Resources
A magazine available from
Maureen Yeomans, 35 Station Road, London, NW4.

Manage Your Time
Sally Garratt   Fontana   1989

Give Us A Break
The role of leisure in women's health and well-being
Erica Wimbush   Routledge and Kegan   1989

Fitness For Sport
Rex Hazeldine   Crowood Press   1985

Getting Firm
Fitness, health and nutrition   Time Life Books   1988

Fully Fit In 60 Minutes A Week For Women
S.O'Sullivan   Thorsons

Work Out That Works For Women Who Work
B. Pearlson   Lindom

Women And Social Security
Federation of Claimants Union FCU 296 Bethnal Green Rd, London E2 0AG

How To Survive As A Working Mother
Lesley Garner   Penguin   1982

The Cohabitation Handbook
Rights of Women, London.   Pluto Press   1984

Organisations

Centre For Stress Management
156 Westcombe Hill, Blackheath, London, SE3 7DH.

OPUS
For parents under stress Tel 071 263 5672 / 071 645 0469

Relaxation For Living
Dunesk, 29 Burwood Park Road, Walton-on-Thames, Surrey KT12 5LH.

British Holistic Medical Association
Gloucester Place London NW1 6DX Tel 071 262 5299

Council For Complementary And Alternative Medicine
Suite 1, 19a Cavendish Square, London, W1M 9AD. Tel 071 409 1440.

British Acupuncture Association
34 Alderney St, London SW1V 4EU Tel 071 834 1012

Traditional Acupuncture Society
1 The Ridgeway, Stratford-on-Avon, Warwickshire, CV37 9JL. Tel 0789 298798.

International Register Of Oriental Medicine (UK)
Green Hedges House, Green Hedges Avenue, East Grinstead, Sussex, RH19 1DZ.
Tel 0342 313106 or 7.

National Institute Of Medical Herbalists
41 Hatherley Road, Winchester, SO22 6RR. Tel 0962 68776.

Register Of Traditional Chinese Medicine
19 Trinity Road, London, N2 8JJ. Tel 081 883 8431.

Society Of Homeopaths
2 Artizan Road, Northampton, NN1 4HY   Tel 0604 21400.

British School Of Reflexology
The Holistic Healing Centre, 92 Sheening Rd, Old Harlow, Essex CM17 0JW   Tel 0279 29060

British Association Of Art Therapists
13c Northwood Rd, Highgate, London N6 5TL

Black Women Healers Group
Wesley House, 4 Wild Court, London WC2B 5AU Tel 071 405 0624

British Alliance Of Healing Associations
Healing Secetary, 26 Highfields Ave, Herne Bay, Kent CT6 6LN Tel 0227 373804

National Federation Of Spiritual Healers
Old Manor Farm Studio, Church St, Sunbury-on-Thames, Middlesex TW16 6RG
Tel 0932 783164

Professional Association Of Alexander Teachers
17, Egglestone Terrace, Stockton-on-Tees, Cleveland, TS18 1JR.

The Wheel Of Yoga
Acacia House, Centre Avenue, Acton Vale, London, W3 7JX.

British Wheel Of Yoga
1 Hamilton Place, Boston Rd, Sleaford, Lincs NG34 7ES   Tel 0529 306851

British Naturopathic And Osteopathic Association
Frazer House 6 Netherhall Gdns London NW3 5RR Tel 071 435 7320

MIND (Coordinates work to improve conditions for those with mental disturbance)
22 Harley St, London W1N 2ED Tel 071 637 0741

Keep Fit Association
70 Brompton Road, London, SW3 1EX. Tel 071 387 4349

Sports Council
70 Brompton Road, London, SW3 1EX. Tel 071 388 1277

British Sports Association For The Disabled
202 Glen House, 200 - 208 Tottenham Court Rd, London W1P 9LA Tel 071 631 3735

Womens Sports Foundation
Wesley House, 4 Wild Court, London WC2B 5AU   Tel 071 831 7863

CHAPTER 5
LIVING ASSERTIVELY

Assertiveness training has become a fashionable activity.

Extraordinary, that something designed with women in mind, is now being heralded as the answer to managers' problems - most of whom are men.

Rather galling when we consider the hardships in the seventies when trying to introduce women's assertiveness training. How the establishment and closed minds tossed it aside as 'feminist rubbish'.

Something good is well worth protecting.

Dangers

Men do have a need for assertiveness training. Assertive behaviour dissipates the negative use of power.

> **However, the dangers inherent in men learning assertiveness techniques are that:**
>
> 1. Some men will not understand the real fabric to assertiveness and will merely use the techniques to further personal power.
>
> 2. Men who are already in powerful positions will and do become even more powerful because of their 'good' interpersonal skills. This may mean the workforce are better treated but, it will also mean that the man WILL ALWAYS hold a leading edge over traditionally disadvantaged groups.
>
> 3. Assertiveness training is culturally bound because it is about behaviour and understanding behaviour familiar to us. White men often do not understand women's culture, or our accepted methods of behaving. Assertiveness training for men can then become a male self indulgence in how THEY perceive the world.

These dangers are actually as applicable for women as for men.

Given that we are all divided on class, race and dis-ability grounds a woman may fall as easily into any of the problems above as men:

1. Some women merely use assertiveness to further personal power.

2. Some women are already holding powerful positions at work and will use 'good' assertiveness techniques to maintain that advantage over other women.

3. White womens' assertiveness training concepts are derived from that bias. Further, white people are not likely to understand black cultures nor the languages and are therefore, uninformed in the accepted patterns of behaviour of black people.

Some Reminders on Assertiveness

Assertiveness training does address power and its use. It is an attempt to equalise power relationships because it was designed with the idea that women are in a weaker position than men. It expects to develop self confidence in women as a way of giving methods of self empowerment in personal behaviour. It also attends to the over-powering person by suggesting that aggressive behaviour is 'not on' and should be actively changed by the individual herself.

Powerful people, like white men and career white women, need to consider how they use assertiveness techniques when involved as the dominant party in interaction. With this in mind, this chapter proceeds with expanding the personal behaviour concepts into the interactive by continually assessing the *context*.

This can be done by broadening our understanding of

CONTROL

The principle here is:

YOU ARE IN CONTROL   :   I AM IN CONTROL

The ACTIVE INGREDIENT is to assume that the relationship we are in will benefit from the other party BEING IN CONTROL in the same way as we will.

For good, equal relationships to work well, BOTH parties need to struggle for that dynamic.

Our perception is lifted from a self-centred one to consider the perception of the other.

Traditional assertiveness training starts us off on a sure footing. Anne Dickson's classic, "A Woman In Your Own Right" gives a thorough and reliable analysis of how to be an 'assertive woman'. (8)

She suggests there are four general types of behaviour which describe the way we relate to others:

1. **Passive** which is characterised by our avoiding taking responsibility for making choices. We may also be inhibited or withdrawn from the mainstream of human activity. We may feel hurt and frustrated because we haven't achieved our goals.

2. **Aggressive** behaviour occurs when we may be too forceful and put other people down. We may be seeking personal aggrandisement and thus belittle others' thoughts and values. It is a behaviour which expects to be superior.

3. **Indirect aggression** is also termed by Anne Dickson as being **manipulative**. It occurs when we are deceitful. It could be a quiet but destructive use of dishonest power. Or it could be a concealed and planned intention to undermine through being anything other than direct.

    Manipulative behaviour may not appear to be aggressive initially because of the deceit involved. However, the result is the same. It will undermine and demoralise others.

4. **Assertiveness** displays us at our 'best' when we are feeling comfortable in ourselves. We feel self respect and respect for those around us. We realise we are ordinary human beings full of contradictions and work towards being open about them as well as trying to 'do better next time'. (9)

Meg Bond's grid taken from her excellent book "Stress and Self-awareness: a guide for nurses" (10), displays the behaviours in a simplified form overleaf:

Summary of the main differences between the four approaches.

	Assertive approach	Aggressive approach	Manipulative approach	Submissive approach
Decision making	Decide on what you think is right in each situation, basing the decision on your own carefully considered priorities, having taken into account those of others	Decide wht is right for you irrespective of others' priorities	Decide what is right for you and pay lip service to other people's priorities. Try to persuade them their priorities are really the same as yours.	Decide according to other people's expectation/priorities with no regard to your own.
Making requests	State what you want/need with appropriate strength of feeling. Listen and enable others to state likewise. Persist when it is important to you.	Demand. Give orders when a request is more appropriate. Blame for not having fulfilled wants/needs in the past. Make threats.	Use insincere ego-boosting to try to get what you want. Try to convince others they really want to do as you want. Try to make others feel guilty. Drop hints. Give the impression that some significant other person wants it (eg. someone in authority). Make veiled threats.	Hold back from stating what you want/need. Grumble because you are not getting it. Fail to consider what you want/need. Make requests in an unconvincing way so the other person does not realise how important they are to you. Give up if the initial response to your request is not positive.
Saying no	Make a clear refusal with appropriate strength of feeling. Persist in your refusal when it is important to you.	Refuse for the sake of refusing. Attack the person for asking. Refuse with inappropriately high strength of feeling.	Try to talk the other person out of their request. Avoid making a direct refusal but give a lot of excuses and side tracks in the hope that the other person will retract the request. Try to make them feel guilty for asking. Cite someone else or a policy as an excuse for refusal. Agree but fail to come up with the goods.	Agree to what you don't want. Initially refuse but in an unconvincing, over-apologetic way and allow yourself to be talked into it.
Giving compliments	Give a clear appreciation with appropriate strength of feeling.	Avoid acknowledging positives about the other person. If acknowledging, do so grudgingly and with complaints about previous negative points.	Give the compliments as though surprised . Infer that there is no need for disapproval at this time, hinting there is at others. Patronise. Use insincere compliments to get your own way.	Hold back from giving compliments. If giving a compliment, overdo it and over-inflate the other person.
Receiving compliments	Accept valid compliments and agree. Reject manipulative compliments.	Demand compliments as your right; attack the person for not giving it before.	Put the credit on to someone else.	Become over grateful for any crumb of approval. Respond as if it's the giver who deserves the praise.
Giving criticism	Challenge what the person has done or said with appropriate strength or feeling. Persist when the challenge goes unheeded.	Attack the personality of the recipient of your criticism. Drag up the past for ammunition.	Become sarcastic. Make jokey put-downs. Hint at disapproval. Make veiled threats. Cite other people's concern or disapproval.	Avoid the person. Grumble or bitch behind their back.
Receiving criticism	Accept valid criticism and learn from it. Reject invalid criticism.	Retaliate. Not listen to valid criticism. Blame someone else.	Try to talk your way out of facing the criticism. Hint it's someone else's fault. Try to talk the other person into changing their mind.	Absorb all criticism whether valid or not. Use it to feed your negative self-image.
Stating opinions	Make a clear statement of your own opinion, not allowing frequent interruptions. Allow others to state their opinions without interruptions and show respect for their right to have their own opinions.	Insist your own opinion is 'right'. Prevent others from expressing theirs. Interrupt a lot. Put other people's opinions firmly down. Show you think they have no right to express their opinion.	Try to convince the other person that your idea is their idea. Try to talk the other person round to your point of view. Make jokey or sarcastic put-downs of others' opinions.	Hold back, not expressing an opinion. If you do express your opinion, do it in an unconvincing way. Allow self to be interrupted and put down. Allow self to be swayed by strong opinions which are really contrary to your own. Seek approval for your own opinions.

The behaviours are merely indicators of a form of human interaction.

> **The concepts are mostly very westernised and come from the need in a capitalist society to make sense of how patriarchy expects women to behave.**

It is evident that many of us do not fit into the stereotypes and so will have a healthy, questioning outlook to 'being categorised'. Our personal behaviour patterns may be defined through our individual struggles against racism, or lesbian oppression, or disablism.

As women we often carry many bag loads of past damage and hostility against us. Our survival response may well be to fight out of corners or carry on fighting from the front. This will be viewed as aggressive behaviour by those feeling attacked. The question is whether we NEED to fight or not. WHAT DEPENDS on it? The Chapter Dealing with Violence clarifies this further.

Our Rights Re-visited

The central theme to assertiveness training however, is the idea of 'having personal rights' and of respecting other people. We have considered how personal power comes in many different forms, in this book. We have also thought about our personal NEEDS which may also sometimes be considered therefore as 'rights'.

> **Rights are only rights if we are all prepared to acknowledge them.**

> **Therefore, amending Anne Dickson's Bill of Rights to include you and I would assist this acknowledgement if it read like this: (11)**
>
> ### <u>OUR</u> BILL OF RIGHTS
>
> 1. You and I have the right to state our needs and set our own priorities as people independent of any roles that we may assume in life.
>
> 2. You and I have the right to be treated with respect as intelligent, capable and equal human beings.
>
> 3. You and I have the right to express our feelings.
>
> 4. You and I have the right to express our own opinions and beliefs.
>
> 5. You and I have the right to say 'yes' and 'no' for ourselves.
>
> 6. You and I have the right to make mistakes.
>
> 7. You and I have the right to change our minds.
>
> 8. You and I have the right to say we don't understand.
>
> 9. You and I have the right to ask for what we want.
>
> 10. You and I have the right to decline responsibility for other people's problems.
>
> 11. You and I have the right to deal with others without being dependent on them for approval.

Looking at the Bill of Rights in this way then demands a further statement WHICH RECOGNISES power differences between the individuals concerned: Indeed the statement should recognise the very power that each individual *brings* to a situation.

Thus, The Bill of Rights might seem safer if this were added to it:

12. **We both** have these rights so long as in pursuing them we do not damage or injure each other or anyone else.

This last premise then starts to take into account the disadvantage built in by oppression because of racism, sexism or any other adverse condition that may occur between people.

> **It more actively accounts for the needs of the disadvantaged individual.**

Both individuals then begin to take responsibility for the dynamic going on between them. It also suggests that one woman can indicate her desire to respect the rights of the other woman. There is also the suggestion that our rights to 'make mistakes' are actually very powerful, and that our decision making around this could hinder the other person.

- The right of a white woman to make a mistake, because of her racism against a black woman is not acceptable - especially if the white woman has the power to NOT make the mistake.

Accepting the 12th point of 'Our Bill of Rights' opens the door to allowing ourselves an acknowledgment of how powerful we are and in what context.

We Are Both In Control

Usually, we do not strive to help another person 'be in control' because we are afraid they will take over and be controlling.

So for instance, if a woman works towards her male partner being in control, too often he may become controlling and she controlled. Society tells us this male dominance and female passive behaviour is OK, which then further cements the problem. Women who are concerned about their male partners' dignity at the expense of their own are not themselves 'being in control'.

They have given up or given away their power.

Being in control means being assertive but it also gives a framework for interaction.

The question is obvious:
BEING IN CONTROL OF WHAT?

THAT is the area for negotiation and THAT is usually where all the tears and strife come.

There seems little point in knowing all the assertiveness techniques if we are not also clear about the boundaries within which we wish to operate, how those boundaries affect other people and whether we are willing to negotiate the change of those boundaries - even if it is against our own personal interest.

Being controlling suggests that the individual wishes to maintain their power base at the expense of the other person.

Being controlled suggests we give up our power base to one who wishes to control.

It is suggested here that any or all of the four behaviour patterns outlined on page 83 may contribute to controlling or being controlled. Unless 'being assertive' is put clearly into the power relationship going on, it may still end up violating the rights of others even when we don't want it to.

BEING CONTROLLING	BEING IN CONTROL	BEING CONTROLLED
"You have to"	"Is it OK for you?"	"If I have to?"

We can distinguish, by the three statements above, the kind of INTENTION an individual presumes when using them.

- We don't have to say **"You have to"** to actually mean it. Silence, looks, body language, explanations, all kinds of attitudes will display **"You have to."** .

All that matters is that the individual assumes the power to tell another person to do something - maybe not necessarily in their best interests. Sometimes the power is thoroughly legitimate - like a parent / child, or manager/ subordinate relationship. Sometimes the power is not legitimate as we realise when we understand classism, racism and sexism for instance.

> **Unless we acknowledge our power base we will never be truly assertive.**

How many of us in this world recognise and are able to acknowledge our power base?

Our response to one who is controlling may well be "If I have to".

- **If I have to what?** Serve your needs, allow you to feel more important than me, do something which depreciates me or gives you power?

The complexity of truly assertive relationships will carry on as long as we interact with one another, depend on each other and expect civilised behaviour.

The final danger of assertiveness training is that an individual may feel she's 'made it' just because she's done her course. Having said that however, many assertiveness teachers display and encourage the true regard for the issues discussed above.

Assertiveness is here to stay and it's important to have the benefit of its principles and strategies. Many women sometimes feel at breaking point for their lack of confidence in these 'cut and thrust' times. Assertive behaviour can unlock a person's true individuality and dignity and allow her to grow and expand - and not at the expense of others.

The following are examples of techniques you will find available to you in most up-to-date writing on assertiveness.

Techniques

Generally, assertiveness training techniques cover these areas:

- Body language and non-verbal communication

- Asserting negative and positive responses

- Techniques in conversation confidence, like how to initiate communication and how to make sure a message is heard.

- Understanding how we can fall into 'compassion' traps

- Being able to express feelings openly - Dealing with put-downs

- Learning how to take criticism

- Disarming anger

- Learning how to listen

- Giving and receiving feedback

All in all these are basic human inter-relationship methods and everyone should be well-versed in them

SO LONG AS POWER BALANCES ARE RECOGNISED.

Recommended Reading

A Woman In Your Own Right
Anne Dickson   Quartet   1988

Stress And Self-awareness
A Guide for Nurses
Meg Bond   Heinemann   1990

When I Say No I Feel Guilty
M. Smith   The Dial Press   1975

Your Perfect Right
R. Alberti and M. Emmons   Impact Books   1974

Assertiveness At Work
Ken and Kate Back   McGraw Hill   1982

Organisations

The Womens Therapy Centre
6 Manor Gdns London N7 6LA   Tel 071 263 6200

Pellin Centre (Feminist Therapy Centre)
43 Killyon Rd, London SW 8 2XS   Tel 071 622 0148

CHAPTER 6
KNOWING OUR BODIES

In this chapter we examine the anatomy of the body purely as a means of both reminder and explanation of how and why it functions. The information is mostly technical and will assist in greater comprehension of other chapters. It is intended to be used as reference material.

If we do not understand basic physiology we are left disadvantaged in knowing what our likely physical limits are. The reader is urged to refer to "Our Bodies Ourselves" (12) for essential information on women's health.

Definitions

The study of the form and arrangement of organs is called **anatomy.**

The method of functioning is known as **physiology.**

The **body** consists of four major axial parts - the head, neck and trunk, the legs and the arms.

These are supported by the **skeletal system**

and are moved by the **muscular system**

which is controlled by the **nervous system**

through stimulation of the **sense organs.**

The body is covered by the **skin.**

Activity is maintained by energy obtained from food dealt with
by the **digestive system**

And released by oxygen obtained by the **respiratory system.**

These materials are distributed by the **blood vascular system**
and by the lymphatic system, which also carries waste materials to be removed
by the **excretory system.**

Hormones are stimulated by the **endocrine system.**

Women have a different **reproductive system** from men.

These are eleven systems of the body and we shall view each one in turn.

(13)

1.The Skeletal System

The bones in the body can be described as a series of connected rods. The design of these connections determine the nature and range of movement between the rods (bones) which are next to each other and their potential functions. Combined, they form the skeleton.

> **The movement at any given joint is made possible by the pull of muscle on bone across the joint.**

Figure 5 - The skeleton

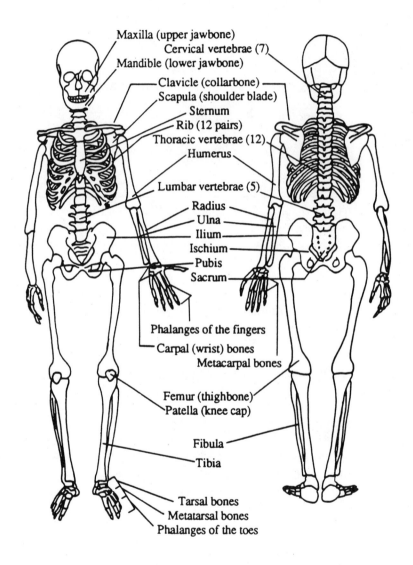

Maxilla (upper jawbone)
Cervical vertebrae (7)
Mandible (lower jawbone)
Clavicle (collarbone)
Scapula (shoulder blade)
Sternum
Rib (12 pairs)
Thoracic vertebrae (12)
Humerus
Lumbar vertebrae (5)
Radius
Ulna
Ilium
Ischium
Pubis
Sacrum
Phalanges of the fingers
Carpal (wrist) bones
Metacarpal bones
Femur (thighbone)
Patella (knee cap)
Fibula
Tibia
Tarsal bones
Metatarsal bones
Phalanges of the toes

The skeleton provides the framework of the body and its three functions are:
   a. Support
   b. Attachment
   c. Protection

a. Support

To provide support for the soft parts of the body and to give it mechanical shape.

b. Attachment

Muscles are attached to the skeleton, allowing movement at the joints brought about by their pulling and dropping bones into different positions.

Tendons - attach the muscle to the bone. Connections between tendon and muscle or tendon to bone are very vulnerable to injury, although the tendon itself is seldom injured.

Ligaments - are bands of white fibrous tissue connecting the bones about a joint. They help stabilise the joint and and are extremely resistant to distortion and stretch. Once stretched however, they keep their new length, having 'plastic' rather than 'elastic' properties.

Periosteum - is the connective tissue around the bone. It has a strong suppporting function and may be incorporated with tendons and ligaments. During the growing years, periosteum protects a layer of tissue containing "bone-growing" cells. It is an unstable material and extremes of muscle fatigue or force of contraction should be discouraged.

Joints - occur whenever a bone or cartilage meets another. They are classified according to the amount of movement possible between the articulating surfaces.

There are three main types of joint:

Fixed joints in which there is no movement, as with teeth and skull.

Slightly moving joints like those between the vertebrae of the spine.

Freely moving which are the majority of joints. These vary enormously in their structures, according to the range of movement. Some, like the knee, allow for a bending action. Others will enable a rotation, such as the shoulder and arm joint, and some rely on each other for a full movement - as in the foot where there are many bones and joints.

c. Protection

The skeleton protects the more delicate parts of the body, for instance the skull protects the brain, the neural arches of the vertebral column surround the spinal cord and the heart and lungs lie within the rib cage.

Cartilage is also known as a shock absorbing or reducing agent. In the knee cartilage discs not only cushion the impact of movement between two bones, but also serve to ensure perfect contact between them. Cartilage has no blood supply and therefore cannot repair itself once damaged. This can become very serious when the joint is arthritic.

However, it seems that the synovial fluid found in a joint provides the cartilage with nutrients. It has been shown that exercise increases the amount of fluid and thus assists in the efficiency of joint movement. Careful exercise may well help arthritic joints.

2.The Muscular System

A muscular system has the capacity to produce movement in the whole body - this includes obvious limb movement as well as movement of certain internal organs.

A muscle consists of a number of contractile or elastic fibres bound together in bundles. The bundles are in turn bound together by a thick band usually spindle-shaped and always contained in a sheath. This sheath is extended at the end to form strong fibrous bands known as tendons, which fasten the muscles to the bones.

Figure 6 - Cross section of muscle

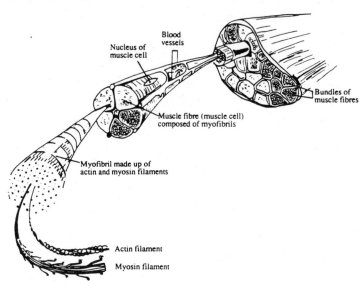

The muscle receives its stimulus from a motor nerve and in response will shorten its length so that, in action a muscle always contracts. Muscles are supplied with arteries to bring them fuel for food and repair, and oxygen for combustion of the fuel. Veins carry away the waste products such as carbon dioxide.

Muscles act by converting chemical energy into mechanical energy, causing pull on the bones and so bringing about certain movement. The specific action will be determined by the type of bone (or lever) it connects and the angle of attachment ie. the type of joint it crosses. The efficiency of each action will be critically affected by the stability and status of each joint.

There are three types of muscle in the body each concerned with a different movement:
   a. Skeletal muscle
   b. Visceral muscle
   c. Cardiac muscle

a. Skeletal Muscle

This is attached to the skeleton either directly or indirectly, and is controlled by the VOLUNTARY parts of the nervous system.

The muscles responsible for skeletal movement have two points of attachment:

-   the point of ORIGIN is the bone to which they are attached and which they DO NOT move.

-   the point of INSERTION is the bone to which they are attached and which they DO move.

The biceps muscle of the arm has its origin (or attachment) at the shoulder end of the upper arm, whilst the point of insertion is in the lower arm bone just below the elbow. Therefore, it is the lower arm bone which is lifted by the biceps.

Skeletal muscles contract quickly and relax promptly. The muscles may become fatigued by prolonged repeated stimulus.

b. Visceral Muscle

This is associated with the viscera - the internal organs such as the thorax and stomach muscle, the abdomen. It is controlled by the INVOLUNTARY parts of the nervous system. The muscles are made up of minute spindle-shaped cells whose fibres are so fine that they appear unstriped. They are thus sometimes referred to as smooth muscles.

Contractions of these muscles are rhythmic and slower than the skeletal muscles and they do not become fatigued.

c. Cardiac Muscle

This is the heart muscle. It is a very tough organ which contracts regularly and in response to the load put on it by the rest of the body. It has characteristics of both voluntary and involuntary muscle in structure. It does not fatigue readily but does so if the heart beat is much increased for a long period so that there is insufficient rest between each contraction.

The heart may become diseased if it becomes 'furred up' with fatty deposits. This can start very early in life and over many years may build up to cause a blockage in one of the coronary arteries. A heart 'attack' will occur, which causes severe chest pain. If the heart stops beating for more than a few minutes death will result.

Taking care of our hearts is part of everyday living. Less fats, smoking and alcohol WILL reduce the risk of heart attacks. Exercise helps keep the heart used to demands. It is a sturdy and faithful muscle. Caring for it is a vote in favour of valuing yourself.

Our muscular system is the base of our personal power.

The use of our energy in muscles creates movement.

Energy = movement = power.

3.The Nervous System

To ignite movement in our muscles we need signals and messages to be taken rapidly to those parts we wish to move.

So long as muscles and nervous system are not damaged we are in the privileged position of being in control of a whole range of complex and versatile reactions. These can range from saving our lives when under threat to an operation as delicate as brain surgery.

The nervous system deals with the conduction of messages in the form of electrical impulses from one part of the body to another. It also coordinates the body's activities.

It has two main divisions:
   a. The Central Nervous System
   b. The Autonomic System

a. The Central Nervous System

This mainly deals with voluntary impulses. It is made up of the brain, spinal cord and peripheral nerves.

i.   The brain

consists of the CEREBRUM which is the grey matter and controls voluntary movement, receiving and interpreting conscious sensations. It is the seat of higher functions such as the senses, memory, reasoning, intelligence and morality.

The CEREBELLUM lies behind and below the cerebrum and controls muscular coordination and balance.

The MEDULLA OBLONGATA connects the brain with the spine. It controls the internal, involuntary processes.

ii. The spinal cord

lies in the canal formed by the vertebrae.

Its functions are to:

- relay impulses coming in and going out at the same level

- relay impulses up and down the cord to other levels

- relay impulses to and from the brain

iii. The peripheral nerves

These connect everything up and come in three forms:

- SENSORY nerves receive stimuli and pass impulses to the spinal cord

- ASSOCIATION nerves relay the messages

- MOTOR nerves pass impulses from the brain and spinal cord, ultimately to affect the muscles and glands.

b. The Autonomic System

This is the sympathetic and parasympathetic nervous system. It supplies all body structures over which there is no voluntary control.

Sympathetic nerves increase body activity like anger and excitement.

Parasympathetic nerves slow down body activity like decreasing heart pressure and secretion of sweat.

We make conscious voluntary decisions sometimes to become angry or excited, but the autonomic system takes over the decisions about body mechanics in response to your instructions.

4. The Sense Organs

The skin, nose, eyes and ears are all sense organs. They convey to our brains sensations from our external environment so that we can make 'sense' of them.

The body is conscious of eight distinct types of sensation:

1. Touch or pressure
2. Temperature
3. Pain
4. Taste
5. Smell
6. Hearing
7. Balance
8. Sight

Touch, temperature and pain receptors are widespread in the skin.

There are three different types of sensory endings which relay information to nerves:

a. *Exteroceptors* which sense stimuli from outside the body

b. *Enteroceptors* which sense stimuli in the viscera.

c. *Proprioceptors* which sense tension in tendons and muscles

We are not usually conscious (though we could become far more) of the enteroceptors and proprioceptors. We do feel 'pangs of hunger' for instance, but it is usually excessive stimulation which causes the pain that we feel.

Stimulation of the enterceptors and proprioceptors set up autonomic reflexes which control such actions as peristalsis of the alimentary canal.

5.The Skin

The skin is made up of two layers of tissue, the epidermis closest to the surface and the dermis which is under the growth layer.

The functions of the skin

a. It serves as a protective cover, against friction, water loss and entry of germs.

b. It regulates the body temperature, the fat in the dermis gives insulation against heat loss. The hairs also give insulation by entangling pockets of air.

c. The sebaceous glands secrete an oily substance called sebum which prevents hairs from becoming too brittle.

d. The sweat glands produce a watery secretion containing salts and waste material and are therefore excretory organs, but their main function is to regulate body temperature.

e. Finally it provides a sensory covering over the entire body by the sensory nerve endings which perceive touch and temperature changes.

Figure 7 - The skin

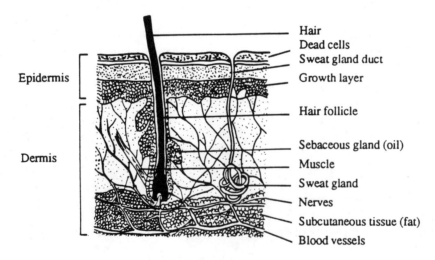

6.The Digestive System

This consists of a long chain of organs which channel food into a variety of receptacles which digest the food through chemical and mechanical action. It is known as the alimentary canal and is responsible for changing food put into the body, into substance suitable for absorption, and therefore usable by the body. This is assimilation.

The health and efficient working of the body is dependent, to a large extent, on the food eaten and the treatment it receives.

The body needs materials for:

- Growth

- Repair

- Heat

- Energy

These are all supplied by the food and liquid we eat.

It is the digestive system which produces the chemical and other changes which make it possible for the food to perform functions necessary to life. It is essential for there to be an adequate balance in the diet of protein, vitamins, minerals, fats, and fibre.

Figure 8 - The digestive system

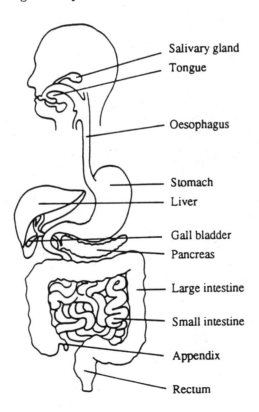

Salivary gland
Tongue

Oesophagus

Stomach
Liver

Gall bladder
Pancreas

Large intestine

Small intestine

Appendix

Rectum

Gaining Back Control

7. The Respiratory System

Respiration obtains oxygen from the air and uses it for the oxidation of food materials to liberate energy. Consequently, it produces carbon dioxide and water as waste materials.

The Structure Of The Respiratory System

This consists of the:

- **mouth and nose** through which air is brought into the body and sent out. The nose and mouth warm the air and saturate it with moisture. Dust and germs are filtered out by hairs in the nostrils and by mucous.

- **pharynx** which allows air to pass from the mouth and nose into the wind pipe via several openings and which in turn takes the air down into the

- **lungs** These are two sack-like structures which make use of the air by allowing for oxygen to be absorbed via very small alveoli into the blood stream. These then receive back from the plasma in the blood, carbon dioxide.

Figure 9 - The respiratory system

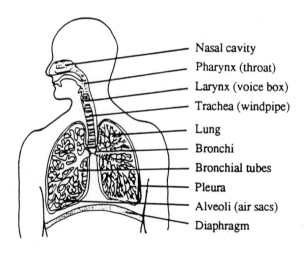

Nasal cavity
Pharynx (throat)
Larynx (voice box)
Trachea (windpipe)
Lung
Bronchi
Bronchial tubes
Pleura
Alveoli (air sacs)
Diaphragm

Breathing

To some extent breathing can be controlled voluntarily but it is normally a reflex action whose rate varies when body activity changes. When running, breathing is faster so that the body can take in more oxygen for the muscles to use. Breathing is very slow in sleep because the body is using minimal energy.

The lungs do not work by themselves. They function through a variation of atmospheric pressure achieved by the muscular action of the powerful diaphragm muscle. The contraction and relaxation of the diaphragm results in an alteration in atmospheric pressure which thus provides a 'sucking' action.

The two actions associated with breathing are:

a. *Inspiration* which sucks in air into the lungs through the diaphragm contracting. It is also achieved through the intercostal muscles moving the ribs upwards and outwards thus increasing the diameter of the thorax. These combined movements increase the capacity of the thorax to receive the air.

b. *Expiration* or breathing out is brought about by an elastic recoil when the muscles relax.

Normally about 1 pint of tidal air is changed at each breath, but additional air can be inspired in and more can be forced out by the use of stomach and chest muscles. This is important to remember when shouting for instance, because the volume of the shout will be dependent on how much air is forced out of the lungs.

8. The Blood Vascular System

Blood is a fluid contained within a closed system of vessels, the arteries and capillaries, through which it is made to circulate by the pumping action of the heart. It is the chief transportation agent in the body.

We shall look at the structure and function of blood first and then the circulation system. The lymphatic system is examined last.

The Blood

Blood appears to the naked eye as a red viscous fluid, but when examined more carefully 55% of it is found to consist of plasma which is a yellow liquid and the rest are cells called corpuscles.

The functions of the blood can be divided into two main areas:
> **a**: Transport
> **b**: Protection

a.   Transport

- Food from the alimentary canal to the tissues.

- Oxygen from the lungs to the tissues.

- Waste materials from tissues to the excretory surfaces, eg. carbon dioxide to the lungs and nitrogenous wastes to the kidneys.

- Hormones from the endocrine glands to other organs or tissues whose metabolism they control.

- White corpuscles to the seat of infection.

- Heat from more active tissue to less active and to the skin for removal.

b.   Protection

- White corpuscles combat invading organisms.

- Clotting stops bleeding from wounds and helps to keep out germs.

- White corpuscles help healing of wounds.

- Salts provide a suitable environment for the life of cells by maintaining constant osmotic pressure and by buffering action.

The Circulation

The blood can carry out its functions only when it is kept circulating in the blood vessels.

The most urgent and continuous need of the tissues is for oxygen. Therefore, the blood passes to the lungs and to the other organs alternately. The heart is completely divided to keep the oxygenated and de-oxygenated blood separate.

The circulation is divided into two principals:
    (a) the pulmonary circulation (to and from the lungs) and
    (b) the systemic circulation (around the body).
    (c) The heart is central to the whole system.

a.   Pulmonary circulation

provides a single artery from the heart which then divides to go to each lung. Further branching takes place to provide finer arteries and then capilliaries. These supply the alveoli. Venules then collect the blood from the capilliaries and join to form larger and larger veins which eventually leave the lungs as the four pulmonary veins. These open directly into the heart.

Figure 10 - The circulation system

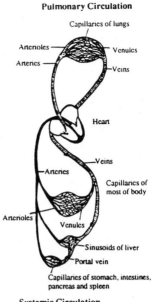

Pulmonary Circulation

Capillaries of lungs

Arterioles — — Venules

Arteries — — Veins

Heart

Veins

Arteries

Capillaries of
most of body

Arterioles

Venules

Sinusoids of liver

Portal vein

Capillaries of stomach, intestines,
pancreas and spleen

Systemic Circulation

b.   The systemic circulation

provides blood to all other parts of the body.

Arteries carry oxygenated blood away from the heart (apart from the pulmonary artery). They have thick elastic walls made up of three layers of tissues.

Veins proceed towards the heart and carry de-oxygenated blood (the exception being the pulmonary vein). They have thinner, less elastic walls. Internally they possess pocket-shaped valves (to prevent blood flowing backwards) .

The pressure of this blood is very low (unlike in the arteries). Smooth flow is maintained by:

- flow of blood from the capilliaries

- pressure from surrounding organs, especialy skeletal muscles

- the pairs of valves

- suction as the thorax expands during inhalation of breath

c.   The heart

is a hollow muscular organ about the size of a closed fist. It lies in the thorax between the lungs and diaphragm. It is divided into four chambers. These are the right and left atria in the upper part of the heart and the right and left ventricles in the lower part.

The right and left sides of the heart are divided by a solid wall or septum, which prevents the de-oxygenated blood coming into contact with the oxygenated blood in the left side of the heart.

Figure 11 - The four cavities of the heart

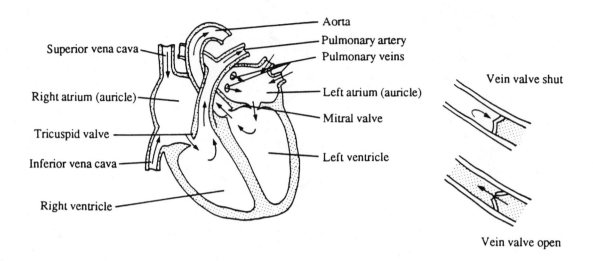

The functioning of the heart:

- The veins empty blood with little oxygen from the body into the right atrium. The blood flows through to the right ventricle and is pumped to the lungs.

- When the blood has become re-oxygenated by the lungs, it is returned into the left atrium. The blood flows then into the left ventricle and is pumped to the rest of the body.

Heart beat:

The heart muscle contracts rythmically with a period of relaxation and rest between each contraction. The contraction period is known as systole and the dilation as diastole. The whole repetitive process is the cardiac cycle.

The average heart will pump 4000 gallons of blood around the body each day.

The Lymphatic System

This system is part of the vascular system, it works in association with blood vessels. The lymph vessels are concerned with transporting excess fluids, wastes and potentially harmful materials. The transported materials will pass lymph glands. There, the bacteria and harmful substances are filtered off and destroyed.

> **The lymphatic system is an important part of our body defence system.**

It is this system which can be undermined by HIV and this could lead to AIDS. The Human Immunodeficiency Virus may be present in an individual's body and they may have no problems related to that. However, HIV may be transmitted to others who may develop AIDS. The reasons for some people developing AIDS while others do not is still not fully understood.

9. The Excretory System

The body needs to rid itself of waste materials, these are:

   a. Indigestible and undigested food residues.

   b. Nitrogenous waste from the breakdown of proteins.

   c. Carbon dioxide from the oxidation processes.

   d. Excess salts.

   e. Water.

   f. Heat.

These are excreted through:

   a. The alimentary canal which removes residues of food, with a little heat and water, through the anus by defecation.

   b. The kidneys remove nitrogenous waste and excess salts not removed by sweating and also excess water not lost through breathing or sweating.

   c. The lungs remove carbon dioxide. Water and heat will also be lost if the inspired air is dry or cold.

   d. The skin removes excess heat not lost through breathing. Loss of heat is aided by evaporation of sweat and some nitrogenous wastes, salts and water.

10. The Endocrine System

The endocrine system consists of a number of glands which secrete chemicals known as hormones into the blood circulation. It is chiefly a regulatory system maintaining internal balance of the whole body. Our hormones can definitely have an effect on the way we feel, our energy use and our sense of well-being.

Some examples of important hormones:		
Hormone	**Endocrine gland**	**Function**
Adrenalin	Adrenals	Raises pulse rate and volume of blood pumped by heart. Increases respiration . Constricts blood to the digestive sytem and skin. Stimulates blood to the muscles.
Insulin	Pancreas	Stimulates the body to release energy.
Thyroxine	Thyroid	Controls growth and release of energy.
	Pituitary	Releases various hormones which regulate growth, and the action of other endocrine glands.
Oestrogen	Gonads	Stimulates the thickening of the uterus wall during ovulation.
Progesterone	Gonads	Prepares the uterus for pregnancy.

The hormones are released as a result of interaction between the conscious and unconscious needs of the body.

We still do not know enough about how much our mental state of mind can affect the production of hormones.

So, for instance, if we are FEELING very low and depressed it is not always clear whether this is the mind keeping the body subdued, by giving messages to the thyroid and pituitary glands. Or, if it is these two glands which decide and keep the whole body lethargic and unenergetic.

One thing is for sure, however. Often, consciously deciding to take energetic action can *re-vitalise* the whole system, like for instance, running. Another hormone then comes into action - adrenalin and nor-adrenalin, which can make us feel far more energised.

11.The Reproductive System

This system fundamentally differentiates women from men.

Our potential to give birth is dependant on the features of this system.

This then pre-determines certain characteristics:

    a. Size and shape
    b. Hormonal cycles
    c. Creation of life

a. Size And Shape

Women are likely to have:

- **hips** which provide enough room for a foetus to grow in, and be expelled from

- **narrower shoulders** which help keep the skeleton balanced

- **height** which may be influenced during the growing years by the amount of protein given to the developing girl

- **breasts** which might provide a baby with milk

- **fat** which is important in times of famine, especially if pregnant

b. Hormonal Cycles

Women are affected by reproductive hormones which provide these cycles in life:

- **childhood** with an absence of reproductive cyles

- **puberty** during adolescence which brings with it body changes and the onset of menstruation

- the **reproductive phase** when menstruation occurs at intervals, often monthly but may be in longer or shorter periods

    menstruation occurs as a result of the shedding of the uterine wall lining. It is not needed for pregnancy. After menstruation, when bleeding has finished, the ovary starts the process of ovulation. An egg matures which is then released as one which could be fertilised. It passes down the fallopian tube to the uterus.

- the **menopause** which draws the menstruation cycle to a halt, usually in a woman's 'middle years'.

- the **old age** phase when hormones may affect us adversely. Some women (often the more wealthy) may take Hormone Replacement Therapy which counteracts certain aspects of the ageing process.

c. Creation Of Life

Women are the child bearers. Our bodies are constructed to nurture the development of a foetus, in the womb, during a nine month period.

Hormonal changes occur during pregnancy which alter the nature of the mother's body to cater for her new off-spring. For instance, her breasts swell and her pelvic tissues begin to soften to accommodate the child's exit.

The uterus (which is the strongest and most powerful muscle in the human body) expels the child with a series of contractions.

Figure 12 Reproductive organs and menstrual cycle

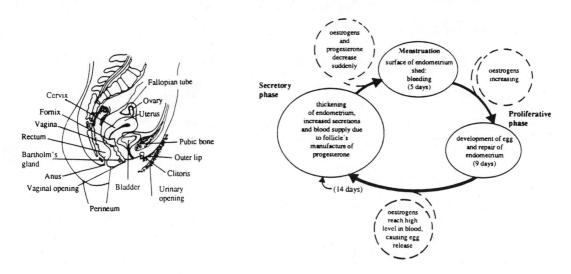

Adapted from "Our Bodies Ourselves"(14) - an excellent handbook which answers most of the questions we may have because of our reproductive system and other health issues.

KNOWING OUR BODIES is fundamental to understanding how much they are capable of. Our body is our most personal space and territory. It is ours and ours alone. Indeed, it *should* be our own.

> **If our body is being misused or abused by anyone else our rights to autonomy and human dignity are being taken away.**

We can also abuse our own bodies. Being physically assertive asks us to be thoroughly aware of how and why we do misuse our anatomy and physiology. Our knowledge recognises the consequences to ourselves of not properly caring about our bodies.

We have to take risks for many reasons.

Sometimes, furthering our comprehension of how our body works helps us to make better decisions about those risks.

Material in this chapter drawn from:

Basic Anatomy And Physiology
HGQ Rowett   Murray   1983

Introduction To Human And Social Biology
Don Mackean and Brian Jones   Murray   1982

Atlas Of Anatomy
Editor: Casey Horton   Cavendish Books   1985

Revise Human Biology
Morton Jenkins   Letts   1984

Principles And Practice Of Physical Therapy
WG Arnold-Taylor   Stanley Thorpes   1982

The Body
Anthony Smith   Penguin   1978

Recommended Reading

Our Bodies Ourselves - A Health Book By And For Women
Angela Phillips and Jill Rakusen.   Penguin   1989

Women's Health; A Spare Rib Reader
Sue O' Sullivan, (Ed)   Pandora   1987

A Womans Guide To Alternative Medicine
L Grist   Fontana   1986

Why Suffer Periods And Their Problems?
Lynda Birke and Katy Gardner   Virago   1982

Curing Pmt The Drug-free Way
Moira Carpenter   Century   1985

Menopause: A Guide For Women Of All Ages
Jill Rakusen Cambridge   National Extension College /
                         Health Education Authority   1989

How To Fortify Your Immune System
Donald Dickenson   Arlington   1984

Avoiding Heart Trouble
Consumers Association   1980

Heart Attacks, Prevention And Treatment
British Medical Association   1979

Beating Heart Disease
Health Education Authority (Free)

Organisations

Health Education Council
78 New Oxford Street, London, WC1 1AH.

Health Education Authority
Hamilton House, Mabledon Place, London WC1H 9TX Tel 071 631 0930

The Womens Natural Health Centre
1 Hillside, Highgate Rd, London NW5 1QT Tel 071 482 3293

British Nutrition Foundation
15 Belgrave Square, London, SW1 8PS.

National Association Of Pre Menstruel Syndrome
2nd floor, 25 Market St, Guildford, Surrey GU1 4LB Tel 0483 572715

Breast Care And Mastectomy Association
26a Harrison St, London WC1 8JG Tel 071 837 0908

Womens National Cancer Control Campaign
1 South Audley St London W1Y 5DQ Tel 071 499 7532

British Pregnancy Advisory Service
Austy Manor, Wootton Wawen, Solihull, West Midlands B95 6BX Tel 05642 3225

The Family Planning Association
27 - 35 Mortimer St, London W1N 7RJ Tel 071 636 7866

Pregnancy Advisory Service
11 - 13 Charlotte St, London W1 P 1HD   Tel 071 637 8962

Brook Advisory Centres
National network offering free counselling for young people.
153a East St London SE17 2SD Tel 071 708 1234

National Abortion Campaign
Wesley House, 4 Wild Court, London WC2B 5AU Tel 071 405 4801

Association Of Radical Midwives
62 Greetby Hill, Ormskirk, Lancs L39 2DT Tel. 0695 572776

Maternity Alliance
15 Britannia St. London WC1X 9JP Tel 071 837 1265

National Childbirth Trust
Alexandra House, Oldham Terrace, London W3   Tel 081 992 8677

National Osteoporosis Society
Barton Meade House PO Box 10 Radsytock, Bath BA 3 3YB

Organisation For Sickle Cell Anaemia Research
22 Pellat Grove   London N22 5PL   Tel 081 889 3300

Arthritis And Rheumatism Council For Research
41 Eagle St London WC1R 4AR Tel 071 405 8572

College Of Health
18 Victoria Park Sq   London E2 9PF   Tel   081 980 6263

Chest, Heart And Stroke Association
Tavistock House North Tavistock Sq London WC1H 9JE   Tel 071 387 3012

CHAPTER 7
PROTECT YOUR BACK AND LIFT IT!

Thinking About Heaviness

What's heavy? A simple answer - everything. All materials have weight.

The only reason we feel weight is because gravity continuously and consistently pulls all matter down towards the centre of the planet.

Gravity is a FORCE.

We do battle with gravity every time we move or lift anything - including ourselves. All objects may be given a weight by using a measuring scale which actually resists gravity. This measurement of resistance informs us of the weight of an object. The bathroom scales give you a reading of your personal weight by resisting the heaviness of your body created by the pull of gravity.

In this chapter we look at:

The notion that **women are 'weak'**

Good posture and balance

How to lift

The weights room explained

Knowing your strength

Women Are 'Weak'

The popular contemporary image of women portrayed by the male media is to display (especially white women) as being weak and ineffectual. This has resulted in many women believing themselves to be unable to lift certain objects.

It is clear that women and men, by and large, lift different objects in this society. There are some fairly obvious divisions between men and women characterised by occupation. Traditionally male dominated industry relies on the physical ability of men to MOVE heavy equipment and objects. Mining, construction and engineering are notable examples. Women have attempted to enter these industries but are still in an exasperating minority, often because men will restrict their entrance.

Some women have illustrated their ability to lift and carry people down ladders in the Fire Service, but have then been so badly harassed by male colleagues they have had to leave.

That sort of experience makes it appear that some women still can't 'make it' - because they are physically inferior.

So, the mythology is reinforced and we become part of it.

When we do lift heavy objects we don't give ourselves the real credit for it. We don't often think:

> "I'm strong because I successfully lift the 35 lbs of my child three or four
> times a day - without injuring myself."

And then, if we have never handled a ladder before we may expect it to be heavier than it is and presume it to be a 'man's' job - even though an aluminium ladder may only be 20 lbs in weight.

> **It is important before attempting to lift anything that we rid ourselves of the stereotypes drummed into our sub-conscious about lifting.**

Nursing may be assumed to be 'women's work' and yet an individual nurse will lift and carry many more human beings than a fire fighter will.

The clearing-out of imagery is necessary because the assumptions behind them are dangerous for our physical welfare. On the one hand we are rendered weak and ineffectual because we can't handle it (what men do) and on the other we are 'naturally' expected to lift children and those who may be ill or have disabilities.

Unless we start with a fresh slate and look at every lift in its own unique character we may end up saying either:

> "I can't do that - because I'm not expected to",

therefore preventing ourselves from being in control of the resources around us, or:

> "I have to lift that (heavy shopping) because I'm expected to"

and perhaps give ourselves an injury because we have assumed it to be something we should not complain about doing.

Our expectation of whether we can or can't lift something prescribes our personal limitations. Looking at objects that have to be moved, with an open mind, allows us the opportunity to judge carefully whether we can manage it or not.

This needs to be done in relation to our analysis of the object, our physical strength and TECHNIQUE. Technique in lifting assumes the correct methods in relation to the way we use our bodies.

We need to identify first how our body works before we can succesfully use it as a vehicle to move objects about.

> **Understanding how the body is best able to function mechanically, allows us then to use it economically and efficiently, with the least possible risk of injury.**

Good Posture And Body Balance

Stability and control is gained by good body posture and balance.

If we lose balance, we lose control.

Movement puts us constantly in danger of our losing control by gravity trying to pull our body off balance.

The body design is to hold up our heavy weight, vertically from the ground.

It is also designed to move our anatomy and the weight of other objects.

Moving the body is always in relation to gravity pulling ANY PART of the body which is not directly in line with our centre of gravity.

The *line of gravity* runs from the crown of the head down through the pelvis to between the feet.

The *centre of gravity* is found in the middle of the pelvis at the base of the spine.

Figure 13

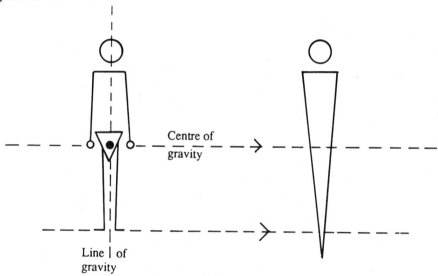

In the above diagram the shoulders are wider than the distance between the feet so an inverted triangle is formed.

Gaining Back Control

In the diagram below the feet apart gives the triangle a base which can stabilise the body:

Figure 14

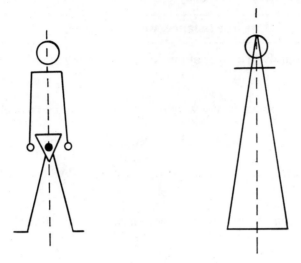

However, we are not just flat pin people; the line of gravity also runs down the side view of the body:

Figure 15

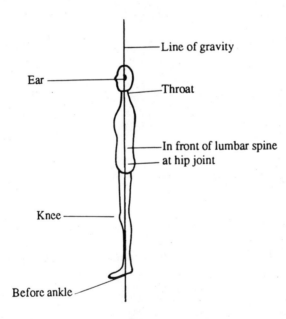

This suggests that widening the feet at the base is not necessarily going to stabilise the whole body.

However, placing one foot forward, bending your knees and keeping your weight in the middle lowers your centre of gravity towards the ground.

This then considerably stabilises the whole body:

Figure 16

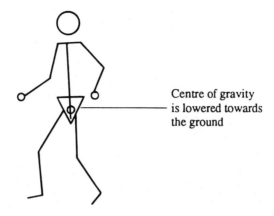

Centre of gravity
is lowered towards
the ground

We know the principle behind a see-saw pivoting two weights on either end:

Figure 17   *Balance*

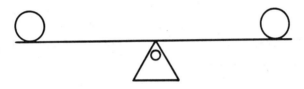

If one is heavier than the other, the lighter weight will rise in the air while the heavier drops down towards gravity:

Figure 18   *Imbalance*

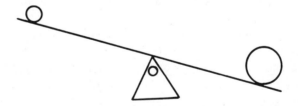

Consider then, the effect of putting out an arm with shopping in the hand, how that will affect the other side of the body:

Figure 19 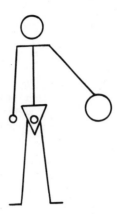 It will feel *unbalanced*

The reaction will be to lift the other arm out, and lean the body over away from the weight to balance up.

However, it will also be easier to carry the shopping if it is CLOSER to the body because then the shopping weight is CLOSER TO THE CENTRE OF OUR GRAVITY:

Figure 20 *Balancing*

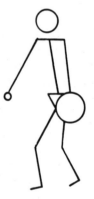

The CENTRE OF GRAVITY is an imaginary point representing the weight centre of the body - usually at the base of the spine. The idea of shopping pulling the body over dramatises the effect of weight pulling at your centre of gravity. In effect the centre of gravity has shifted from the pelvis outwards - towards the heavier weight.

> **It is easy also to forget that our bodies are themselves heavy.**

The average head for instance, weighs around twelve pounds. Put it in a position away from the line or centre of gravity and it will pull the body off balance. The reason we don't fall over when tilting our heads however, is because a variety of muscle groups work hard to hold us up.

The problem arises though, when we habitually keep our bodies off balance because we have poor posture. What happens then is that some muscle groups are over worked, holding you together, while others are left under used.

We weaken muscles by not using them, or using them incorrectly.

Then, when we come to use the muscle in an activity we do not often engage in, the weaker muscle may not be strong enough to cope and it will tear. Far too many 'bad backs' are caused through muscles being left to waste away chronically. Sometimes even an unusual movement like raising the arm can tear a back muscle.

To understand this fully we need to examine these areas:

a. How muscles move the body through using levers.

b. How muscles work and complement each other.

c. How posture aids a healthy protection of the back and whole body.

How Muscles Use Levers

We have learnt in chapter 6 that the body's skeleton is a frame, consisting of a number of bones held together by ligaments. The reason for the body remaining upright is because muscles hold the levers firmly together through their capacity for tension and relaxation. The bones are rigid, often rod-like structures while the muscles are flexible. To make two rods move muscles on either side pull them together or apart.

The rods act as levers on each other and use junctions (the joints) between the bones as pivots, see on the following page:

Figure 21 illustrates:

1. The two arm bones:

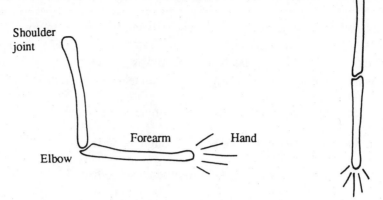

2. The forearm is pulled up towards the shoulder by the biceps muscle which contracts to raise the lower bone:

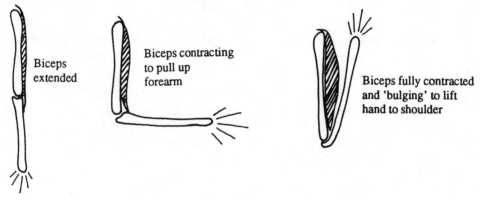

3. Whilst it does this the triceps, on the other side of the bone relaxes to accomodate the biceps action:

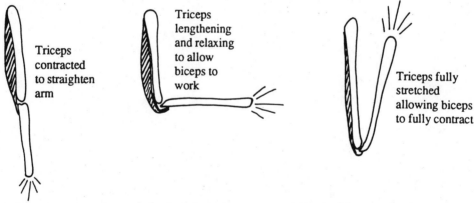

4. To extend the arm out straight again the triceps contracts while the biceps relaxes:

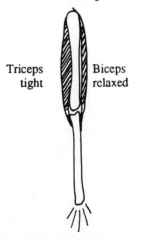

Muscles Working Together

Figure 22 describes how muscles complement each other through what is known as antagonistic functions - they do the oppposite of each other.

To make sure that muscles are able to work effectively they should always be viewed in their relationship to each other. So, active exercise of the biceps should always be followed by as much exertion on the triceps. Otherwise we end up with bulging biceps and weak triceps which are unable to support us when pushing ourselves up out of the bath.

However, the body is marvellously constructed to perform many series of complicated movements and therefore muscles must also work together in groups, for instance, walking involves the muscles of the lower leg, the thighs and those in the bottom. The body is also stabilised by back and stomach muscles.

The abdomen group of muscles are of major importance because they protect the back. Their length and depth across the stomach region hold up our upper body which thus assist the back muscles.

Figure 22 illustrates muscle groupings:

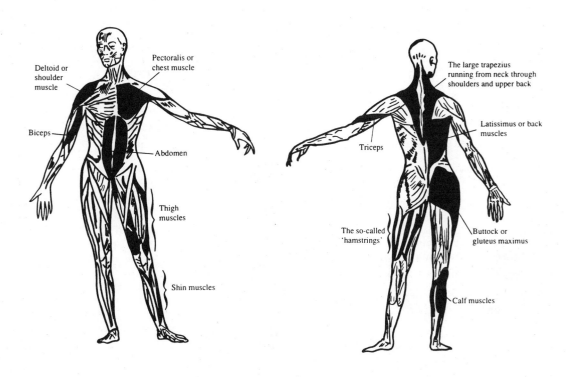

Posture Aids Strength

Good posture protects the back, the neck, head and also internal vital organs.

We have already seen how the line of gravity runs down from the crown of the head, through the pelvis to the foot immediately in front of the ankle.

Posture aids us in lifting any object because we are constantly reminded that we should keep the weight we carry (our own and external objects) close to the centre of gravity and the line of gravity.

The most central part of our bodies is the spine and looking at the figure below it is clear that from the front and back it should appear thoroughly perpendicular.

Figure 23   FULL VIEW

The VERTICAL line
is very apparent here

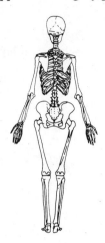

However, from the side the spine has two curves. These curves and the large number of vertebrae (thirty three in all) provide a shock absorbency which far exceeds a rigid structure. Its flexibility also allows for mobility within an enormous range.

Figure 24   SIDE VIEW

A good upright posture.
The line of gravity runs down
from the crown of
the head, through the hip,
middle knee & to the heel

(15)

Good posture protects this extraordinary design by allowing all the muscle groupings to act in favour of an erect and perpendicular pose which carries body weight symetrically.

It's worthwile working at getting your posture right. Few of us do have good posture.

Watching yourself in the mirrror especially from a side on view gives useful insight into what you're doing with yourself. Alternatively find a friend to straighten you up.

The basic standing posture considers these aspects:

a. The feet are parallel, slightly apart and pointing forwards.

b. The body weight is distributed evenly through the legs with the hip joints placed directly over the knee joint.

c. The knee joint is relaxed and not rigid, to accomodate body weight.

d. There is a natural curve in the lower back, but the abdomen is tight and clearly being used to support the trunk.

e. The pelvis is tilted in towards the abdomen thus assisting the abdomen in its work.

f. There is another natural upper back curve which is supported by the shoulder muscles drawing the shoulders in line with the pelvis.

    Tension in this area is produced by the muscles having to work doubly hard in maintaining a 'drooping' posture!

g. The neck holds the head steady without letting it loll into the chest or letting it drop backwards to the shoulders.

    It is useful to think of yourself as having an invisible wire pulling your head up into your line of gravity.

Gaining Back Control

Figure 25

This is how we can
get round shoulders

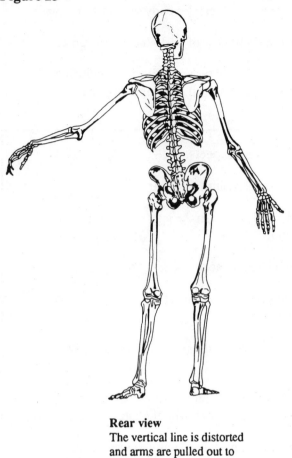

Rear view
The vertical line is distorted
and arms are pulled out to
reduce "toppling"

Side view

Figure 26

Imagine the spine as a pile of books, see how much stronger and more stable the separate components are if stacked properly.

Original Drawing by Sarah Blight

Lifting

To lift something from the ground we are dealing with a number of different concerns:

a.   Our EXPECTATION of moving the object
     (or not moving it as the case may be).

b.   The SIZE of the object.

c.   The BULK of the object.

d.   The SHAPE it has.

e.   The WEIGHT or actual heaviness of it.

f.   The PLACE we are going to put it.

g.   Our BODY'S ability to move the object.

Before lifting anything unusual go through the above check list and ensure that you have answers for each stage. There's just no point in grabbing articles and 'hoping for the best'.

Remember, with lifting ANY object our main concern is to keep it as close as possible to our centre of gravity. Aided by a correct posture the weight will also be close to the line of gravity.

Figure 27

To take weight from the ground upwards we have a number of choices. We could lift it with our arms:

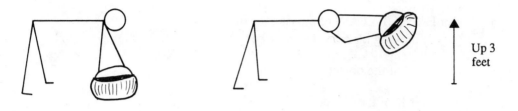

We could lift it with our arms and trunk:

We could lift it with our LEGS:

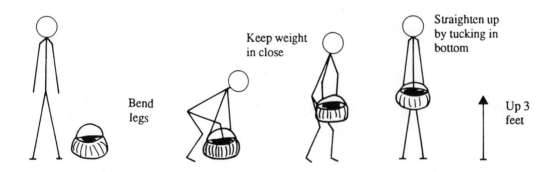

It is evident from these diagrams that the safest method of lifting is to use the powerful leg muscles to take weight up from the ground. Using the arms to keep the weight CLOSE to our body ensures the proper use of our body mechanics.

> **These are the basic elements of lifting objects:**
>
> a. Think that the object to be lifted is an extension of your body.
>
> b. Remember that you will be using the object for only a particular period of time.
>
> c. Remember constantly the see-saw effect of your line of gravity in association with your centre of gravity.
>
> d. Make a decision about where you place your body in relation to the weight.

The Weights Room Explained

In a weights or conditioning room you will find one or all three of these items:

Free weights

Machine weights

Cardiovascular equipment

The best weights rooms has all three types of equipment so that you have the opportunity to condition all aspects of your muscle and cardiovascular systems.

Free Weights

> **These are commonly found in two forms:**
>
> a. Dumbells - small sized weights which may be held in each hand, and of varying heaviness.
>
> b. Barbells which are rods - perhaps 5 or 6 feet long to which you can attach two collars to fix your desired weight at each end.

They are called 'free' weights because you are free to move them in relation to your body IN WHATEVER ACTION you decide.

> **They provide an excellent opportunity for you to become stronger in relation to the action of your lifting which has to be controlled entirely by your own decision making.**

Therefore, it is essential to have training in the use of free weights so that you are thoroughly aware of how to lift them and in what sequence.

There is a clear danger in using free weights because:

i.   You may attempt to lift something too heavy and strain muscles.

ii.   You might drop something too heavy - perhaps on your own body.

iii. You may train 'out of correct alignment' to your proper posture position and thus deform your anatomy.

For these reasons rigid machine weights have been designed.

Machine Weights

These are found in most gyms these days for three reasons:

a.   They are safer and do not require you to undergo such rigorous training in how to use them as do free weights.

b.   They are therefore more convenient and easy to use.

c.   They somehow seem 'more exciting' than the free weights - a tremendous amount of prestige goes into marketing the most sensational machines which can - "change your life."

Of course, we know that only YOU can change your life, but somehow the machine can make it all seem so much easier. This is not only the effect of shining chrome, gadgets and devices but also because your experience on the machine can be *more comfortable* than with free weights. It is more comfortable because you have the illusion of being in control of the weight.

In fact YOU don't, the machine does because IT HOLDS THE WEIGHT RIGID while all you do is propel it upwards IN A STRAIGHT LINE.

The machine takes over your responsibility **to control the direction of travel.**

The different types of machines fall roughly into four categories:

i.   Lifting weight from one position UPWARDS like the bench press which has a bar which has to be pressed UP from the chest.

Figure 28

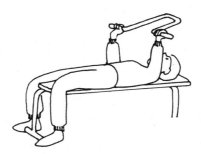

ii.   Pulling weight DOWN like the latissimus pull where you pull the bar down from above your head to your chest or behind your neck.

Figure 29

iii.   Using the weights in an OUTWARDS / INWARDS motion like the 'Pec Deck' where the weight is distributed so that you pull it from an open arm stance to a closed one.

Figure 30

iv.   Using the weights HORIZONTALLY so that your body pushes weight away from it like the leg press where you sit to push the weight from a bent knee position to a straight leg.

Figure 31

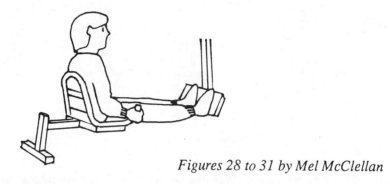

Figures 28 to 31 by Mel McClellan

The use of these basic movements is then further differentiated by which parts of the body you may want to condition. So, you may want to strengthen your calf muscles by pushing weight UP from standing on to your tip toes. The weight is placed on your shoulders. Or, you may wish to strengthen your upper leg muscles by pushing the weight supported on your shoulders UP from a semi-squatting position to full standing.

There are many different types of machine weights and they come in all shapes and sizes. Some manufacturers of rigid weights seem more sympathetic to shorter people using them than others. Universal equipment is often 'within reach' of an average sized woman. However, even so there still appears to be flagrant neglect in basic measurements such as grasp, width and length of arms and length of the trunk.

It is important to analyse critically what you find in a weights room and if the equipment is not designed for your stature either be extremely careful or don't use it. DO complain!

Cardiovascular Equipment

Every good gym will have something which will allow you to both warm up and condition your breathing and blood system. Usually there will be a bike (perhaps with measuring devices on it so you can see what calories you are using.). There may also be a rowing machine, a 're-bouncer' which is like a small trampoline or a treadmill for running.

If there is nothing in the gym for you to warm up on and get a 'good puff going' then an old fashioned jog round the block is essential. You could achieve the same effect by skipping.

Appendix 1 has further information on weights rooms and their equipment.

Using The Weights Room

DO REMEMBER it is essential to go through a warming up period before
using weights:

Stretch

Warm up by running, skipping, cycling or bouncing

Stretch

NEVER use weights from cold. Your muscles won't like it and you are in
danger of tearing them even on weights you may be used to.

Then AFTER you have finished with the weights, COOL DOWN by:

Stretching again

Putting on some warm clothes

The weights room was once a male preserve, promoted and maintained for men by
keeping a macho image of how weights are used.

However, different types of weight training produces quite different effects.

Here are three examples of how the weights room may be used:

i.   **General fitness**

Toning muscles so that they become more efficient in action, using
lighter weights.

ii.   **Specific fitness**

Concentrating on sports related training. Weights are used specifically to
complement your sport.

iii.   **Body building**

This increases muscle size to get desired proportions in the body, either for your
own personal benefit or to go into competition.

The way women use weights rooms is often dependent on at least five factors:

   i. If it is a place to be comfortable in because it is

- clean

- light

- not smelly

- the right temperature

- men do not harass you

- the floor is properly covered

  ii. If the staff are sympathetic and well informed

 iii. If guidance and support is given

 iv. If the equipment is right

  v. If the times are right

Naturally a lot of these factors are also some which men feel concerned about too.

The most important point for women however, is whether they are made to feel welcome.

Don't allow yourself NOT TO BE!

Strengthening muscles through weight training puts us in much better shape to cope with the ordinary needs of everyday lifting.

It also trains and disciplines you to think about weight and how best to move it.

It is one of the best methods of getting to know your real body strength.

Knowing Your Strength

We have learnt that good posture allows us to keep our body

IN BALANCE

It is evident that many of the effects of stress and of poor health are due owing to the body being

OUT OF BALANCE

For us to maintain good balance we need first to understand how our posture affects our well-being.

Secondly, we can then understand better how we can put ourselves in to jeopardy if we do not keep correct posture when lifting or carrying.

We have extended our thinking in this chapter to examine how we are able to be more powerful because we can use our bodies to move objects. We use our energy physically to transport ourselves and objects. This action provides us with power. Having personal, physical strength is something we all have. The only DIFFERENCE is that some of us are stronger than others because we use our functioning muscles more efficiently.

It is suggested therefore that each of us can always strengthen those functioning muscles in our bodies, to the level of strength we want them to have. Remember, there are 656 muscles in your body, and even if some are so damaged they cannot work it is still likely that there are others which can be strengthened even more than you think.

> **There is ALWAYS capacity in the human body to become**
>
> **STRONGER**

We need to reclaim our strength as a part of personal power, without shame or defensiveness.

Without knowledge of our physical strength we severely disadvantage our ability to be in control of our physical environment.

Recommended Reading

Neck And Back Problems
The spine and related disorders
Jan de Vries   Mainstream   1987

Getting It Straight
The Norris Technique of Body Alignment
Patricia Norris   Bantam   1986

Back In Action
Straight Answers to Back Pain and its Relief
Sarah Key   Bantam   1986

Banish Back Pain
Effective Self-Help with the aid of simple home remedies
Roger Newman Turner   Thorsons   1989

Understanding Back Trouble
A Consumer Publication WHICH?   Consumers Association   1988

Back Fitness The Yoga Way
Karen Zebroff   Thorsons   1980

New Ways To Health : A Guide to Chiropractic
Swan Moore   Hamlyn,   1988

Lifting, Handling And Helping Patients
Patricia Downe and Pat Kennedy   Faber   1981

Weight Training And Lifting
John Lear   A & C Black   1989

Weight Training For Women
Mary Southal & E G Bartlett   David & Charles   1986

Getting Stronger: Weight Training For Women And Men
Bill Pearl   Shelter   1986

Circuit Weight Training - Effective, Flexible Training Plans For Fitness, Health Strength And Stamina
Tony Lycholat   Thorson   1989

Anatomy For Artists
Leonardo Collection II   Prisma Editions

Athletic Ability And The Anatomy Of Motion
Rolf Wirhed   Wolfe Medical   1984

Organisations

British Chiropractic Association
Premier House, 10 Greycoat Place, London, SW1P 1SB. Tel 071-222 8866.

College Of Osteopaths
110 Thorkhill Road, Thames Ditton, Surrey, KT7 OUW. Tel 081-398 3308.

National Back Pain Association
31-33 Park Rd, Teddington Middlesex TW11 OBA

CHAPTER 8
EARTH, WIND, FIRE AND WATER

In this chapter we think about being outside. Being without shelter. Having no physical structure to protect us from our environment other than that which we might be able to carry.

In these islands being outdoors may mean finding ourselves in one of many varied and distinctive settings.

It could have any or all of the features of:

- an ocean
- a coast
- an estuary
- a river
- a swamp
- a lowland area

- a highland area
- a mountain
- arable land
- a woodland
- a lake
- a snowfield

These features can provide enjoyment, interest and satisfaction. They can also all impart such hostility that we might die in them if we have not protected ourselves. Surviving outside is the ultimate challenge because it means we are relying on minimal resources. We have to be consistently and constantly conscious of ourselves in relation to the environment.

Most of us are protected from the reality of environmental force. We have built a standard of comforts about us which virtually ignores the power of the elements. It certainly is worrying to think that high wind, flood and drought may destroy our shelters and standard of comforts.

Unless we appreciate how fragile our protection is we endanger ourselves.

This chapter is divided into two:

The Challenge of Survival

Danger Expected

The Challenge Of Survival

What Is There To Survive?

The Environment Itself

The broad descriptions of the types of environment that may be found are listed previously. Each of them will provide distinct characteristics arising out of the geology that defines it. It is useful to understand their separate characteristics because they yield knowledge of what to expect from them.

We know that a swamp will be virtually impossible to cross because it will suck us in. We know that the coast will be subject to tidal change and we may therefore be cut off by water. Having an extensive knowledge of the geographical features equips us with what to expect from the area we are in.

Apart from this static approach however, we need also to be aware of the changing elements that might occur at anytime depending on the time of year and altitude.

The elements:

- Temperature

- Wind

- Movement of water

- Movement of soil or land

- Rain

- Snow

- Sun

- Dryness

- Light

- Darkness

When we are outside any or all of these eventualities can occur. All of these are dictated by the weather, except for light and dark and earthquakes. The sun of course affects it all. An inert landscape without the influence of weather would be extremely boring. Thus, we have an extensive variety of challenges in Britain and Ireland.

Our Physical Needs

The fundamental need to be satisfied at all times for survival is to keep our body temperature at the right level. In response to this need we build shelter and make clothes for ourselves to wear.

If we take this primary need and keep it like a compass in our heads all the other elements of personal survival fall into place:

- The need to not get too cold, ie to not die of hypothermia

- The need to not get too hot, ie to not die of sunstroke or thirst

---

We therefore require:

- Food to maintain energy and body temperature

- Water for metabolism and sweat

- The right temperature for muscles to function

- Protection of the cardio vascular system by not subjecting it to an extreme of temperature like cold as this may cause shock and seizure

---

It may all sound obvious but when you've climbed the hill on a beautiful summer's day, the clouds gather, the rain falls and suddenly you're lost, having regard for your temperature needs is paramount.

If you have the correct suppplies with you you'll be alright.

Problems

Which brings us to coping with problems in the environment we find ourselves in.

We can separate out two forms of problems:

- Expected

- Unexpected

If we haven't got ourselves sorted out we may be rudely awakened by the environment destroying our illusions of it.

Figure 32

WHAT HAPPENS WHEN THE ENVIRONMENT INTERFERES WITH OUR ILLUSIONS ABOUT IT

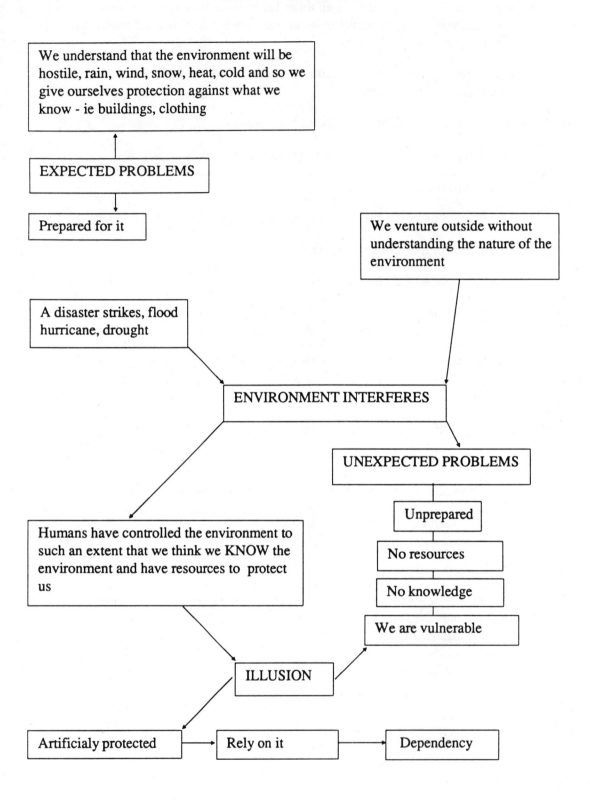

Basically, a problem arises when we haven't properly prepared ourselves for it. Usually, the ENVIRONMENT INTERFERES with our expectations. This is either because the weather has provided some phenomenon to deal with or, we have put ourselves in a place which may suddenly become threatening - a swamp, or the tide comes up or we have to get over a barrier of some sort.

Usually, when we're outside we want to get from one place to another - often to a shelter.

If the problem is that the weather has changed attend to your temperature needs as a priority.

If the weather creates a barrier, for instance a flash flood, then here are some guidelines to work through.

These will also be true of any barrier you might encounter outside ie a river, a mountain, a gorge.

Overleaf are some guidelines for overcoming barriers:

GUIDELINES FOR OVERCOMING BARRIERS

ATTITUDE	If your attitude is negative "I can't get over it" you deny yourself the opportunity to try to overcome the difficulty.

"I can try" gives these opportunities:
- Revitalises
- Energy is restored
- Provides a reason to go on
- Gives belief
- The barrier itself provides a challenge

BARRIER	Because the barrier becomes a challenge you can:

- View it as a whole object

- Ask questions about it

- Look at it from all angles

- Consider the barrier as components of the whole

- See if parts of the barrier may hold answers to the whole

RESOURCES	Your own

Others

Physical around you

In relation to the barrier and its components

ANALYSE	Put different discoveries into different:

- sequences

- combinations

Match your knowledge base to the new discoveries

ADAPT	Yourself and your resources to what your next move will be
IDENTIFY	Fall back positions
TRYING	Keep on!

TURN something *INTO* something else!

Thus, your arriving at a river which needs to be crossed on your journey becomes more than a barrier. It is a challenge.

- Your desire to get over it provides a reason to do so.

    You break it down into components - it moves, it's fast, it's deep, it's ten feet wide, the banks are safe, there is a sturdy tree overhanging it.

    You consider your knowledge and are sure that the tree would support your weight and the bank has vegetation which clearly suggests stability.

    You have a rope with you.

    You use the rope on the strongest overhanging branch.

    You swing across the river.

    The problem has been overcome.

Accidents

Sometimes problems turn into accidents. There is a difference between the accident which happened because it was coincidental (you happened to be under the tree as it fell) and an accident where we created the circumstances for it.

Sometimes the division is blurred. If we heard the tree creaking and the trunk bending and still we walked under it, then we might suppose that we actually risked the accident. If we had no knowledge of trees, we may be oblivious to the danger signalled by their creaking and swaying.

> **Still, who caused the accident? Ourselves or the tree?**

It is of course, unrealistic to attempt to anticipate all the possible accidents that could happen while we are out in the wild. What we can do is make informed judgements and guesses about the nature of the dangers ahead. Being outdoors and moving through an unfamiliar environment is a risk-taking activity.

Accepting our vulnerability first, then ascertaining how many illusions we are living with about the nature of the environment and finally making decisions about using it, helps us to understand the risks we take.

Sometimes it is important to learn the hard way, take risks and find out for ourselves what we are capable of by doing it. There are so many things that can go wrong outside that worrying constantly about risks will take away the enjoyment of your activity.

> **There is a balance between:**
>
>   challenge : risk : excitement : completing

If an accident happens and you are on your own go back to the guidelines for getting over barriers. The barriers will be your immobility, probably your pain and then the danger from the elements.

If you are with companions all of you should use the guidelines - especially so in a mixed group of men and women. Men may have a completely different notion of how to overcome the problem. It is sadly all too often reported by women that their male companions outdoors too readily resort to brute strength before using their minds to make an informed decision.

> **Don't let anyone be hasty in decision-making.**

What Is There To Learn?

Knowledge

> **To recap, the knowledge which will protect you outdoors falls into these categories:**
>
> - the type of environment, its features and characteristics
>
> - the weather and its effect on the environment you are in
>
> - the way resources can be used to provide you with protection or assistance.

Personal Needs

Learning about yourself outdoors is a constant delight if viewed positively. Outside it's just you and basic survival.

The learning to survive more easily and therefore more comfortably consistently motivates.

> **These are the areas to keep learning about:**
>
> - your personal reactions to discomfort
>
> - your personal fitness and stamina levels
>
> - your personal ability to overcome problems
>
> - your personal access to resources which will protect you and knowing WHAT THEY ARE - ie. clothing, boots, compass etc.
>
> - your personal need for challenge : risk : excitement : completing

Change

Learning how to cope with change is a personal need but is worthy of this separate mention.

Because the weather constantly imposes change, and because you will be moving through differing environments, there will always be something new to face. It will vary from the most breath taking and beautiful to the bleakest and most hazardous. Unless we learn how to adapt to these changes we will not be equipped. We might allow despair or distress to overcome us too readily.

Making a decision about how many changes you can cope with then directs you towards how many risks you are prepared to take. It is always better to start off at a level you are already familiar with before proceeding into the unknown. Risks are then more calculated.

> **This then allows you to feel and behave as an individual in control of your own destiny, no matter how short or varied it is.**

Through all this however, you must be sure of the goal you want to reach and what your fallback positions are if you cannot attain it. That sort of flexibility depends on your being able actively to think change, look forward to change and use it to benefit yourself.

It is really learning to live with the unexpected - happily.

Why Do It?

- It prevents you from ever taking your environment for granted

- It creates personal opportunities for change and learning

- It opens up access to territory which is as much yours as anyone else's

- It demands a respectful relationship with the resources around you

- It keeps you fit

- It prompts you to ask questions

- It can be exhilarating

- You can measure yourself against a perfectly legitimate challenge

- One is nearly tempted to say it builds character but ...

  your reasons for being outside are valid and may carry on for many a page. Knowing what your reasons are helps you make decisions in the way you use the environment.

Danger Expected

The call to outside challenge is an invitation to danger. How we cope with the hazards relies on us being thoroughly physically assertive. We need to be knowledgeable of our emotional and physical reactions, and of our abilities and attitude to the situations in which we find ourselves.

Often we participate in outside activities BECAUSE the element of danger produces excitement and a tremendous sense of satisfaction because we accomplished what we set out to do.

Danger does mean there is a real threat to safety. It is expecting danger and all its associated complexities which helps us minimise risk.

> **We do not need to live in fear of the hostile environment if we use our skills to protect us.**

Fear will be part of our experience outdoors because it is that which can make it so exciting. It depends on the level of fear you wish to introduce by making decisions in expecting it and therefore the environment which you choose to furnish you with excitement.

If you have never climbed a mountain before and you decide to go up one you are likely to endure a great deal of fear. The hazards of the unknown and of your reactions to them will probably be very uncomfortable and the risks will therefore be as high as the mountain itself.

It is having an informed understanding of the dangers which will assist all outdoor activity.

We consider how to expect danger at three levels here:

- Using equipment
- Using information
- Being with others

Using Equipment

We can divide outside activities into two sections:

Those which rely on *you* solely as a means of mobility

Those which rely on specialised equipment to aid mobility

Equipment For Yourself When You Are The Means Of Mobility

Your personal equipment requirements will depend a lot on the type of activity you will be engaging in, where it will be and what the weather conditions are going to be like.

On the following two pages are check lists of questions you need to ask yourself before embarking on an activity - to minimise risks.

So, for instance, if you are planning to do some long distance hill walking (no. 2 on grid) then you will want to ask yourself "What kind of footwear, clothing and hand protection do I need? Also, will I need head protection and equipment to carry other articles, and will I be likely to be out at night?" If you cannot answer the questions for yourself you will need to find out the right answers. The next section on using information will then help you.

Figure 33

What kind of equipment do I need when I am the sole means of mobility for:

Activity

1 Gentle walking

2 Long distance hill walking

3 Rock climbing

4 Jogging

5 Pot holing

6 Swimming

Activity	Equipment	Does it need grip	How hardy? 1 Least 4 Very	Should it give support?	Does it need to protect me against:			What weight? 1 Light 4 Heavy
					Water	Sun	Cold	
1	Footwear	✔	3	✔	✔		✔	3
2	"	✔	4	✔	✔		✔	4
3	"	✔	2	✔				1
4	"	✔	3	✔				2
5	"		4	✔				4
6	"							
1	Clothing		2		✔	✔	✔	3
2	"		3		✔	✔	✔	3
3	"	✔	2			✔	✔	3
4	"		2					1
5	"		4		✔		✔	4
6	"		3				✔	
1	Hands		2		✔		✔	2
2	"		2		✔		✔	2
3	"							
4	"		2		✔		✔	1
5	"							
6	"							

Figure 34

Activity

1 Gentle walking

2 Long distance hill walking

3 Rock climbing

4 Jogging

5 Pot holing

6 Swimming

Activity	Equipment	Does it need grip	How hardy? 1 Least 4 Very	Should it give support?	Does it need to protect me against: Water	Sun	Cold	What weight? 1 Light 4 Heavy
1	Head Protection		2		✔	✔	✔	2
2			2		✔	✔	✔	2
3			4		✔	✔	✔	4
4			1		✔	✔	✔	1
5			4		✔		✔	4
6								
1	Carrying Equipment ie.		2		✔			2
2			4	✔	✔		✔	3
3	Rucksack, Belts and	✔	4					4
4	Ropes		2			✔		1
5		✔	4					4
6								4
1	Night Equipment		2					1
2			4		✔		✔	1
3								
4			2					1
5								
6								

Activities Which Rely On Equipment to Aid Mobility

It is when we come to analyse the types of equipment we can use to aid our mobility that we realise how dependent we are on them.

But, this is where those with disabilities can enjoy the outdoors in every way. The equipment aids mobility *for everyone*. People with certain disabilities may require particular adaptations to equipment for personal comfort but probably not too much.

All women suffer the disadvantage that equipment will have been made for the stature of a larger male bulk.

However, the lightness of some women could make up for this disadvantage.

Given equipment designed for women, we could so easily excel in every way.

- The MAIDEN, and her all women crew have displayed this admirably by not only being the first all women crew to sail and complete the gruelling Whitbread Challenge, but also to win two of the six laps, of the Round the World Race.

  Her crew was no doubt lighter than their competitors and the yacht was designed by the captain with her team in mind.

It must be upsetting for men to discover women CAN DO IT.

The activities we are looking at here are those which expect a high degree of involvement in the propulsion of the equipment.

You will need to have skills in these areas:

- ability to direct

- speed of reaction and movement of directing limbs

- coordination

- balance

- complete knowledge of the craft and its capabilities

- thorough knowledge of the environment you are using and its effect on the craft

- a love of speed

Horse riding is included because it can be enjoyed by women with an extremely wide range of disabilities. Although a horse is not equipment or a craft, the rider still has to attend to all of the above.

You will see on the grid chart below that the equipment actually allows you to use it as if it were *an extension of yourself.*

Normally, the equipment will give virtually no protection against the elements except that which it is designed to move over.

This makes it all the more exciting!

Figure 35 ACTIVITIES USING EQUIPMENT TO AID MOBILITY

Activity	Equipment	Sensitivity to Direction	Allows Grip	Gives Support	Gives Protection Against			
					Water	Sun	Cold	Weight
Cycling	Bicycle	✓	✓	Seat				Light
Canoeing	Canoe	✓	✓	Seat	Under-neath			Light
Dinghy Sail	Dinghy	✓	✓	Seat	Under-neath			
Wind Surfing	Surf Board	✓	✓	Feet	Under-neath			Light
Skiing	Skis	✓	✓	Feet			Under	Light
Hang Gliding	Hang Glider	✓	✓	Trunk		Over		Light
Horse Riding	Horse	✓	✓	Seat				

It is empowering for ANY OF US to learn the techniques of using mobility equipment.

It is absolutely clear that WE have to be in control and that WE have to decide how to use it. Direction is the first consistent challenge. Coupled with speed we can experience the most astounding exhilaration.

Using Information

Sources of information build your knowledge base, some are essential for survival.

Essential

Maps	. . .	Ordinance Survey one, and two and half inch to the mile give all the information needed about terrain.
Compass	. . .	Gives immediate direction to aid map reading.
Weather forecast	. . .	Gives anticipated weather conditions which might raise risks.
Understanding weather patterns	. . .	Gives personal decision making about immediate dangers and in likely near future.
Observation	. . .	Gives immediate analysis of terrain to cover. Binoculars can help.

Background Information

Books	. . .	Read up on the subject.
Clubs	. . .	Join and receive information from newsletters, periodicals, meetings and sharing in activities.
National Organisations	. . .	Which can protect your interests, as well as keep you informed and up to date.
Specialist Shops	. . .	For specialist advice and purchasing equipment - but separate out the sales patter!

Being With Others

There are good reasons to participate with others in the great outdoors:

Learning

Sharing

Celebrating

To achieve these quality experiences we need to be with other people who will engender the conditions for them to happen.

If we are participating with anyone who is competitive, thoughtless, brutish or threatened by our success we will have to do battle against it.

The environment is enough. We don't need people bringing us down outdoors - not until we are thoroughly accomplished anyway. It is important therefore to be selective about who you are outdoors with. The last thing you need is for somebody else to jeopardise your safety.

Learning

Most of us will learn how to survive outside through the help, wisdom and assistance of other people. It may occur in childhood, or it may start or continue in adulthood.

Our friends and relatives may help us learn.

Often though, if we wish to specialise in a particular area we will need the assistance of those who are skilled *both* in the subject and *as teachers*. For all the activities which use mobility aids that expertise is essential.

Here are some points to remember when seeking teaching facilities:

-   are the facilities safe, adequate and well-thought out ?

-   are the teachers sympathetic, welcoming and open?

-   will you start at the level best suited for you?

-   do the teachers ensure that you and your fellow particpants respect each other as well as the environment?

-   do you feel comfortable and if not is the discomfort a natural part of the activity or created by other people?

-   do you want to return to the next session?

-   are you progressing?

If any of your answers disturb you ALWAYS put your personal safety FIRST. EVEN if it means getting out of the canoe and standing on the bank.

Secondly, once you are feeling physically assertive again, COMPLAIN.

Do this to the people who you think will listen and change something:

   - the group leader
   - the manager
   - the club secretary / chair
   - the national organisation
   - the newspaper
   - the local radio

Try also to find someone else who can support you and try, try to KEEP ON LEARNING!

Learning with those who give you hope, confidence, spirit and determination is a joy. We should look for the best and also provide our own resources to help others to gain such quality.

Learning with others is as constantly changing as the weather, and as exciting. It never stops and is always expansive.

Sharing

Learning is part of sharing, but when outdoors in a group, team work and individual motivation has to be balanced and understood.

A good sharing group can provide these assets:

Emotional:

- Support through difficulties - Motivation

- Movement towards the same goals

- Fun, laughter and enjoyment

- Companionship

- Socialising

Practical:

- Varied knowledge and expertise

- Sharing of tasks

- Greater capacity for good decision-making

- Safety in numbers - especially if there is an accident

Once again, if you are not finding these qualities in the groups you are with, ask yourself if it is the best group for you.

Either change it or start another group!

This may also be true for partner work.

Celebrating

Once you've finished the expedition you'll want to rejoice!

If you've been out on your own it will be good to celebrate with others who are aware of the difficulties and hardships you will have encountered. Select these people carefully. You don't need anyone who is going to drop you down from your own personal heights of achievement.

If you're out with other people the whole affair can be a celebration because that's why you're out there in the first place. If the weather's good and you've pitched yourself correctly so that you aren't in too much discomfort, it should be wonderful! Being able to celebrate the wonders and beauty of nature and terrain with others as it happens, can be extremely gratifying.

Enjoying all the sensations of our environment, hot, cold, wet, dry and the interest of the land/seascape is basic human delight.

Nurture the right conditions for yourself, your companions and EXPLORE!

Recommended Reading

The Making Of The English Landscape
WG Hoskins   Penguin   1976

The Natural History Of Britain And Ireland
Heather Angel   Michael Joseph Ltd   1981

Waterways And Water Life Of Great Britain
Heather Angel and Pat Wolseley   Peerage Books   1986

The Uplands Of Britain (Collins concise guide)
Michael Marriott   Quintet Publishing   1983

Discovering Britain And Ireland
National Geographic Society   1985

Walking In Britain
Sue Seddon   Youth Hostels Assoc   1988

Let's Walk
Mark Linley   Meridian Books   1988

Land Navigation: Route Finding With Map And Compass
Wally Keay   Duke of Edinburgh's Award   1987

The A To Z Guide For Light Travellers
Clive Tulley   Writers Block   1988

Survival
Martyn Forrester   Sphere Books   1987

Eddie Mcgee's Complete Book Of Survival
Eddie McGee   Stanley Paul   1988

Come Hell Or High Water
Clare Francis   Sphere Books   1977

Clouds From Both Sides
Julie Tullis   Grafton Books   1986

Tackle Orienteering
John Disley   Stanley Paul   1982

Pathfinder Map Series
Ordnance Survey

Bartholomew Maps And Guides Series

The Usborne Book Of The Countryside (For children)
Usborne   1985

Doe's Directory Of Bus Timetables (Essential for route-planning if using buses)
Travadvice, 25 Newmorton Rd, Moordown, Bournemouth, Dorset. £2.00

Bus And Coach Operators (lists 2000 across the country)
Networking Dept. English Tourist Board free

Organisations

English Tourist Board
Thames Tower, Black's Rd, London W6 Tel 081 846 9000

Field Studies Council (Has 9 research and educational Centres across Britain)
Montford Bridge, Shrewsbury, SY4 1HW Tel 0743 850164

Ramblers Association
1-5 Wandsworth Rd, London SW8 2LJ Tel 071 582 6878

Youth Hostel Association (Open to all ages)
Trevelyan House 8 St Stephen's Hill, ST Albans, Herts AL1 2DY Tel 0727 45047

Countrywide Holidays Association
Birch Leys, Cromwell Range Manchester M14 6HU

National Association For Outdoor Education
50 Highview Rd, Grays, Essex RM17 6RU

CHAPTER 9
HEALTH AND SAFETY

Facing an outdoor challenge makes us realise how dependent we are on resources to protect us.

In this chapter we consider:

Defining a standard of comforts

  Types of built environment

    Our values determining how we build our environment

      Who has influence over our built environment

> **Our health and safety in the late 20th century usually depends on a man-made, built environment and machines, and garments - often woman-made and too often man-designed.**

Defining A Standard Of Comforts

Our standard of comforts is defined by the availability of resources to protect us physically and make us feel 'at home'. The commodities we own will also lend their convenience in satisfying our 'needs'.

Often, useful possessions will help to cut down the time we have to spend in doing particular activities. They also make the whole task less arduous, if not thoroughly labour-free, and will allow the completion of the task to be far more efficient.

So, a washing machine does the job quickly, with virtually no labour involved, and very efficiently. It is a 'modern convenience' which allows us time to do other activities.

> **The less labour-saving gadgets we are able to use the more we have to work physically to gain satisfaction of needs.**

Our standard of comforts is also determined by our personal mobility and access to using a vast range of services within the built environment.

There is nearly always a relationship between our standard of comforts and the level of health and safety we experience.

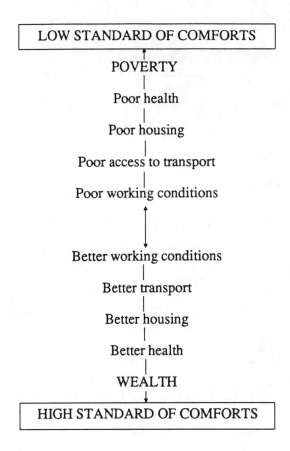

The more money we have the more we can choose to purchase goods which help us feel more comfortable.

> **We have gone beyond a 'Standard of Living'.**

A standard of living suggests an image of raising ourselves above pure survival level. The phrase is deceptive because it assumes that we are *entitled* to raise our standard of living. It assumes our righteousness in our quest for a better and better 'quality' of life.

A standard of comforts better describes the state of human luxury that abounds in our over-fed society. Most of us have comforts readily available, some have much more than others. Our personal comforts are important to us because we are living in a very materialistic age.

If we are honest, we are forced into an appraisal of HOW comfortable we are. Those who are homeless are mostly living at survival level. We are living in a society which punishes some of its citizens by restricting their comforts or denying them comforts altogether.

The evidence clearly demonstrates that the poorer you are the more there is a likelihood of your dying young.

- Between 1971 and 1981 20% of the 'richer classes' health improved, whilst in the poorer classes it got worse.

  10% of the richer classes are people with long term illness whilst 30% have such illness in the poorer classes.

  The long-term unemployed are 19 times more likely to attempt suicide than those in work.

  Over 50% of the richest class participates in sport whilst only 18% of the poorest do.

  6 million homes in Britain are damp.

  In 1985 more than 9 million people lived on or below supplementary benefit level. This increased by 25% from 1981. (16)

Some of us therefore, are still trying to gain a 'standard of living' which takes us above survival level. Others, more well endowed, are living with standards of comfort which are both luxurious and opulent.

Our health and safety is very dependent on the resources we have available to us. One of the most obvious areas of life which assists us in keeping healthy is our built environment. It will protect us from the elements.

There are big problems however, when we consider this from a woman's point of view:

Types Of Built Environment

Our living and working environments in the west are built primarily with these interests in mind:

ENVIRONMENT BUILT FOR AND BY MEN

a. Economic Environment

This is designed by men for the interests of rich men.

It is built by poorer men.

Examples of this environment are banks, seats of government, factories and big transport systems.

Rich men's 'women' may benefit from those parts of this environment that they are 'allowed into'. Even so, women, by and large, have been restricted access UNLESS they are part of the workforce, and therefore containable.

Women are still subject to the male methods and expectations of using the economic environment.

Poorer people generally don't have much to do with this environment other than 'trip over it' or have to work in it.

b. Community Environment.

This is also designed by men for the interests of rich men and for the means of keeping poorer people in their place.

Buildings for community use are for example, churches, leisure facilities, shops, local authority establishments.

Rich men's 'women' will enjoy some of the elitist community environment because thought will have been given to the times when men want to share their sense of community with women.

Women generally, are more likely to use certain community facilities because sexism requires women to 'do the shopping', take the children to school and go to the health clinic.

Poorer people will be provided with inferior facilities and less likelihood of getting out of their communities because there will be less transport available to them.

c. Living Environment.

This is also designed by men but for most of the population. There is every intention of segregating the rich and poor.

Rich men's homes are usually provided with large areas of space in and outside the building.

Rich men's 'women' will benefit from this allocation of space because they will be using the home also. Naturally, how she uses this space will depend on how 'liberated' she is.

Poorer people's homes are designed on the basis of their economic living level. They will be smaller, have less space and less conveniences associated with them.

The richer the individual, the more likely the living environment will provide space between houses, and also between streets.

In all these areas of life the DESIGN of the built environment will not have been controlled by women. All women do, however, live the consequences of the design.

It IS a man-made world.

There are women architects, town planners, designers and economically powerful women. However, they are in a minority and either have to follow male methods or fight very hard for small gains.

One obvious impact of women campaigning is in the provision of child care facilities. However, we are all painfully aware of how little our environment caters for children and those who care for them.

We do have more playgrounds in parks and children are viewed far more like real people now, but STILL it is insignificant compared to the real NEED. Our built environment has been created by men with men's needs in mind.

- How many times have you felt the shelf is just too high or the kitchen is just all the wrong way round? Or the door to the shop could open so much more easily or the street lighting could be improved?

Our cities and towns have also been designed for the economic culture of the west too. Our housing especially, has been built for a world view of small, nuclear families. There is little choice in physically organising living arrangements differently.

We could go through all the different ways that the built environment impedes and demoralises us. However, it may, at this point be more beneficial to think about how our environment would be **IF WE DESIGNED AND BUILT IT.**

It is important to look back at all the mistakes and complain endlessly but why not do some free-thinking and wonder at how it all might be if **WE HAD THE POWER (RESOURCES) TO DECIDE.** Let's enjoy some day dreaming (and it's only through having dreams that we can envisage a future that's different).

What would be important to us in the:

- economic environment?

- community environment?

- living environment ?

And how would we build it?

Our Values Determine How We Build Our Environment

Since it feels too complicated to think about re-structuring everything we presently live with we will need to answer some questions first.

1. What values do we hold dear to us?

```
┌─────────────────────────────────────────────────────────────────┐
│                                                                   │
│              WHAT'S MOST IMPORTANT TO US :                        │
│                                                                   │
│  Community          .........................    Individualism    │
│                                                                   │
│  The social and                    The individual is              │
│  collective                        encouraged to look after       │
│  provision of welfare              her/himself.                   │
│  is emphasised.                                                   │
│                                                                   │
│   Socialism         .........................    Capitalism       │
│                                                                   │
│  Public interests                   Private interests             │
│  and a more controlled              and 'free' enterprise are     │
│  economy are most important.        most important.              │
│                                                                   │
│                                                                   │
│  Need for People    .......................     Need for Machines │
│                                                                   │
│  Caring for others                  Concentrating power and       │
│  and equalising the                 wealth into the hands of      │
│  distribution of wealth.            a few.                        │
│                                                                   │
└─────────────────────────────────────────────────────────────────┘
```

2. What WOULD our values be in building a new environment?

3. What would the top priorities be in deciding what comes first above everything else?

```
┌─────────────────────────────────────────────────────────────────┐
│                                                                   │
│    Go down your local streets and ask yourself these questions:   │
│                                                                   │
│       How SAFE do I feel as a woman, a black person, a woman with │
│       disabilities, a lesbian, a carer of children, an older      │
│       person?                                                     │
│                                                                   │
│       How HEALTHY is it for me?                                   │
│                                                                   │
│       How USEFUL am I / can I be in my home, community and where  │
│       I work?                                                     │
│                                                                   │
│       How USEFUL is my home, community, workplace to me?          │
│                                                                   │
│       What COMFORTS have there been designed for me?              │
│                                                                   │
│       How much ENJOYMENT do I get from my home, community,        │
│       workplace?                                                  │
│                                                                   │
│       What NEEDS does my home, community, workplace satisfy for   │
│       me?                                                         │
│                                                                   │
│       How much CHOICE have I in changing things around me?        │
│                                                                   │
│       Then, ask the same questions for the people who are         │
│       dependent on you.                                           │
│                                                                   │
└─────────────────────────────────────────────────────────────────┘
```

If your answers are horrifying it's because our built environment mostly is HORRIBLE!

However, if some of your answers are favourable, hold on to them because we'll want to keep the good things.

Turning these questions around then, we can ask ourselves, and let's think BIG:

How would my environment be for me to feel:

SAFE in it,

HEALTHY, USEFUL, COMFORTABLE in it,

I can ENJOY it, my NEEDS are satisfied

and I can have CHOICE in changing problems?

Believing that things can change moves us towards expecting, assuming and organising those changes. Unless we have dreams about how it could be, we will not make the most of the changes that ARE likely to occur in the future.

Unless WE have some ideas on how it should be, only the old-guard interests will prevail. It is a political forum BUT, we may be surprised at how much we can influence the design of buildings.

- Twenty years ago dropped pavements were mostly built for the convenience of car owners.

  We are now finding so many more everywhere for use by wheelchair users, buggy-pushers and those who find steps a difficulty.

Safety in our built environment is an interesting concept.

Safety, from what?

Usually, we will find that we need to be safe from the very environment which has been built to protect us. If something is dangerous it is because somebody has designed or constructed it badly or maliciously made it dangerous, or not kept it in good repair.

Rather than the environment interfering with us (like the wind, rain, snow etc) WE interfere with our environment. We don't get it right. We haven't taken into account how people might use resources and what dangers we can create for ourselves.

- A building designed for large crowds may be safe from the elements and comfortable for its occupants. However, a dropped cigarette could cause a fire and the whole structure might go up in flames.

  The responsible people will not have adhered to fire regulations. Everyone's lives were in danger.

Who however, was responsible? The person dropping the cigarette? The partner who saw the cigarette drop but didn't bother to pick it up? The owners of the building? The authorities for not checking fire exits?

The law attempts to say that we all are - especially when we are at work. Even so, a hearing will try to place responsibility somewhere and it may be the difference between the owners not having a NO SMOKING sign displayed and the smoker seeing a NO SMOKING sign and still lighting up.

Who Has Influence Over The Built Environment?

Local Authorities

   Business

      Trade Unions

Local Authorities

Our local Council has far more influence than we usually imagine.

> **The decisions elected councillors make will have a direct effect on the quality of your local environment and even sometimes on your personal health and welfare.**

The local authorities have statutory duties laid down by Central Government, which they are obliged to uphold. Some councils take the 'spirit of the law' at its best and try hard to enhance their districts, so that residents gain the most from their payment of poll tax.

However, the council is restricted by its budget. Although it is expected that everyone pay the same average poll tax, in reality the need for services in some areas is far greater than in others.

Those districts which are economically poorer usually have greater demands for services. Councillors are often only too aware of the need their constituents display, but are limited in satisfying them because they will have a fixed budget to administer.

Even so, they will make priorities around what they perceive to be the most important services requiring finance.

Local people do have great potential to make their feelings heard. Community action, lobbying local councillors, using the media to publicise issues and generally making a noise can all contribute to a Council responding with far more sympathy.

The powers of Local Authorities are to provide:

Housing

This may come in the form of Council Housing; Hostels for those who are homeless; Sheltered or Adapted Housing for older people and people with disabilities and possibly Home Improvement Grants for home owners living in Housing Action Areas or General Improvement Areas.

Vast Council Estates have been built across the country. Some of these have been 'thrown together' by architects who have no understanding or care for the people who will live in them.

> **Inevitably, women will suffer the most from such poor design.**

Countless tenants' organisations exist to keep the Council aware of their needs. Perhaps women need to make more of an impact on what their particular concerns are and make it clear that male council officers have to change their outlook on life.

Planning

The Planning Department will have powers to decide on how land is used in their locality. This ensures a coordination in how districts are developed and structured. There are usually very strict guidelines about how people may build property and how they may use it.

This function of the Local Authority is often only understood in a piecemeal fashion.

- For instance, a neighbour may wish to build an extension to their home and you will be consulted about that. We may not even assume that we have any power at all to influence a decision. But, of course we do and should take advantage of this if needed.

However, we often don't realise how much influence we might have over the planning of the whole district we live in.

The Planning Committee can make decisions about new factories, shopping areas, leisure facilities, about almost everything that MIGHT happen. Local residents can exert tremendous influence over these decisions. The local paper normally advertises planning applications.

Building Standards

The Council will have powers over building standards to ensure safety and correct design.

If you believe a building is unsafe, find the responsible officer at your local Council and complain.

Cleansing

This could cover anything from the provision of public toilets to the removal of graffiti from walls. Refuse collection from our homes is one service we will all benefit from.

However, keeping the environment clean is often a job that goes unnoticed, and will include street cleaning, waste bins emptying, drain maintenance and the cleaning of public buildings.

Without these services our nation would soon be overrun with rats, disease and strife. Give credit where credit is due. If it is a good service, say so. If it isn't, form an action group.

Environmental Health

This function of the Local Authority is an important 'catch-all' which ensures the safety of citizens in the environment as a whole.

If you are concerned about any public health issue you will be able to complain to a Public Health Officer. You may be concerned about out of date food being sold at a shop, or you may have become ill through eating at a restaurant. You may be worried about vermin or pests, there will usually be help if you look for it.

Transportation

The duties here include the provision of an adequate and safe local road system in conjunction with the Department of Transport. It also maintains roads, footpaths and can create cycle lanes. Any improvements being made to roads will have been decided by the Local Authority.

Expecting those improvements to be sensitive to your needs and mobility asks you to make your expectations known and felt.

Some Local Authorities still maintain a transport system - usually buses - for the general public. A low cost, easily accessible service seems idyllic. Transporting people who do not have access to a car is very low on the agenda of a Central Government which has consistently undermined efforts to provide a quality service.

Education

The Local Authority builds schools and makes decisions about the environment in which children will learn. A spacious, warm and inviting environment helps children to relax and enjoy their education. Unfortunately, many Authorities have to cope with old and sometimes dangerous buildings.

Government decisions to 'starve' state schools is indicative of ruling interests keeping those who are poorer, impoverished in their opportunities to learn and improve themselves. Even so, the Local Authority will still administer a massive budget for education.

Social Services

These are one of the least 'built environment' orientated services, although all social workers work in buildings. Usually, Social Services Departments employ large numbers of staff to cater for personal services in the community.

> **These will include:**
>
> - Protecting children at risk of abuse
> - Providing the elderly with personal services
> - Caring for those with physical or mental handicap
> - Giving services to those recovering from a mental illness
> - Providing homes and hostels for any of the above people

Unfortunately, the need is universally greater than the provision and often social workers are over-stretched and frustrated. However, you may believe these services could be better organised and many pressure groups exist to make their voices heard.

Recreation And Leisure

The Local Authority may provide local leisure facilities for the public.

> **These could be:**
>
> Libraries
> Sports Centres and Playing Fields
> Museums
> Parks
> Tourist attractions
> Art galleries
> Theatres
> Large halls for entertainment
> City farms
> Youth centres
> Neighbourhood centres

Whatever it is, the built environment is going to have an effect on the way you use it.

If the Library has steps, heavy doors and turnstiles to go through then you are unlikely to want to use it if you are in a wheelchair, pushing a buggy or carrying heavy shopping.

> **If the above facilities are designed without you in mind then the Council has seriously let you down.**

- If, in the local park, shrubs have been planted with no regard to your safety as a woman, or to the safety of children, then you may not feel comfortable in using the park.

- If, at the Sports Centre, no creche has been provided and there is nowhere for you to relax, you may not feel as welcomed as the man who enjoys his pint at the bar after his exercise.

Leisure is one area in Local Authority provision which is growing. With this comes many opportunities to influence the design of facilities - from the beginning. Unless decision-makers hear from women they will not attend to our needs. WE keep missing all these opportunities.

Consumer Protection

Councils are mandated to enforce a wide range of legislation aimed at fair trading and consumer protection.

Fraudulence and selling goods in a misleading manner can all be taken up by your Local Authority. However, your Council cannot act if it is not given information. You are an important source of information and if you feel you have been unfairly treated by a shop or business someone at the local Council might be able to help.

Some Authorities provide Consumer Advice Services which help prevent problems in the first place. Take advantage of them.

Public Protection

We often take it so much for granted that emergency services will be available for us when a crisis hits.

The Local Authority has influence over:

The Police Force whose duty it is to "Protect life and property, maintain order and prevent and detect crime".

The Fire Service whose duty it is to " Make provision for fire fighting purposes and to make arrangements for giving advice to prevent fire, restrict its spread and provide adequate means of escape."

Although these forces have obviously to comply with legislation, the Council will have authority over priorities and planning of the force. If it is of no interest to the Council that some of its citizens are suffering from racially motivated crime, then they will not put any priority into either preventing or detecting it. If car theft is felt to be a priority then officers will be deployed to combat these offences.

The general public *can* have influence over the way the local police force operates, through the Council system. It is *always* worth letting them know if you are unhappy in the way the police are operating in your area.

Economic Development

Many Councils now operate advice services and schemes which promote economic development in their areas.

Knowing what your authority offers will give you indication of growth and development.

With growth comes change. With change comes opportunities to make an impact on how it all may turn out to be.

USE YOUR LOCAL AUTHORITY TO MAKE CHANGES

Business

Modern business and commerce often like to think they are 'environmentally sound'. More and more now we need to continue the pressure of our own good common sense.

It is important to remember that the Local Authority can exert pressure over commerce in any of the ways outlined above. Without Local Authority intervention business might take advantage of everything that came its way. We could end up with ugly, sprawling buildings, possibly polluting the environment even more than they do now.

If a local business is starting something new in your area you can always find out more from their Public Relations Department. With 'green' currently fashionable, you may be able to influence the business to do far more for you and your community, just because they are becoming more sensitive to the fact that consumers may boycott them if they are environmentally unsound.

These are the major reasons for business to affect our environment:

-   Business has to operate from **buildings**, they may be
    part and parcel of our environment or they just should not be there.

-   Usually **people** will be employed in or around the buildings and
    this will have a bearing on their safety.

-   Business produces a **product** which must be sold to create profit.
    Sometimes the profit motive interferes with health, safety and environment.

-   The end result of producing goods will be also to create a **waste** problem.
    This aspect of modern life is now impinging on our environment so
    threateningly that some people are warning of irrevocable damage.

Trade Unions

The trade union movement, which has nine million members - even though it has been brutally attacked - can also hold answers.

Unions can powerfully influence employers to keep their actvities within the law. It is essential for women to interpret their own working conditions in terms of safety and hazard.

●   If we have a short build and have a workplace designed for men then we will
    probably find a lot of our environment difficult.

    Seats may be too high, giving us back ache. Windows may have latches out of reach
    so we have to teeter on a chair to adjust them.

    Storage may be too deep for shorter arms and therefore unusable. Machines may have
    been designed for a bigger hand span or reaching distance.

These sorts of issues will be very evident for women entering male dominated industries. However, employment which traditionally attracts women will be full of hazards also. Men will have designed machines and processes which they do not anticipate having to use themselves. Women then have to learn the hard way.

- Word processing brings with it the danger of damaging vision. It took a lot of headaches and complaints before employers recognised that operators needed 10 minute breaks every hour. Even so, women may still not take these for fear of not finishing work in time.

  Repetitive Strain Injury is caused by workers having to repeat the same movement for many hours. Too often it is women who are doing these monotonous jobs.

A Trade Union can protect its women members from danger at the workplace by insisting that the law is adhered to.

The Health and Safety at Work Act, 1974 (17) makes clear provision for employers to:

- make the workplace safe
- keep dust, fumes and noise within safe levels
- ensure plant and machinery are safe and that safe systems of work are adhered to
- ensure that articles and substances are moved, stored and used safely
- provide healthy working conditions and adequate welfare facilities
- give staff information, training and supervision necessary for their health and safety
- draw up a health and safety policy statement
- report certain injuries and cases of ill-health to the local authority
- provide first aid facilities

There are also additional specific duties for employers which cover a vast range of circumstances, for instance:

- cleanliness
- correct heat, ventilation and lighting
- the provision of well-maintained sanitary facilities
- dealing with overcrowding
- passages and stairs must not be blocked
- maintenance of plant, machinery and lifting apparatus
- adequate precautions against explosion or flammability
- the provision of free protective clothing

If women are in male dominated work they will probably not be given adequate protective clothing.

- Women working in Parks Departments consistently complain that their footwear is too large for them. The jackets too big. The trousers completely ill-fitting and hand wear dangerous in its looseness.

Is it any wonder that women do not succeed easily in these industries when they are physically in danger and feeling uncomfortable? It is imperative for Unions to take on these problems and for women to be active in defining what is right and wrong for them.

The 1974 Act gives ample scope for much leverage to change working conditions. It is a LAW and an employer does have to abide by it or face legal charges.

> **We do not often enough take employers to task**
>
> **to ensure our own safety.**

The 1974 Act is however, very interesting in its ideology. It calls also for ALL employees to fulfill their duties under the Act.

> **These include:**
>
> - taking reasonable care for your own health and safety
>
> - taking reasonable care of OTHERS' health and safety also
>
> - cooperating with your employer on health and safety
>
> - not interfering with anything provided for your health and safety

> **The Act therefore asks us to be an ACTIVE PARTICIPANT in the interests of our own health and safety.**

It is a very interesting concept since we are all too often completely oblivious to the real dangers around us. The Act certainly asks us to be far more responsible for ourselves and others than we often are. It asks us to be aware.

> **Perhaps we need to adopt this ideology into our whole lifestyle.**
>
> **After all ... who DOES care about the health and safety of women in our society?**
>
> **AND *WHO* WILL HAVE TO INSIST ON THE CHANGES?**

Women are meant to be 'RETURNING TO WORK'. From what one may ask? However, each of us will hold some influence over her own job.

> **IT IS TIME TO BE CLEAR ABOUT THE POWER INHERENT IN THIS NEWLY FORMING WORKFORCE.**

Women do not have to follow the old methods. Industry, our economy, our very national psyche calls out for change and new ideas. We COULD catch the moment and use our increased influence by thinking **people** first and EXPECTING the environment to satisfy our human needs.

HOW DO WE DO IT?

Imagining what might be is the first step.

Second, is checking base with other women.

Third, believing.

Fourth, taking risks.

Fifth, completing.

GOOD LUCK AND <u>EXPECT</u> IT TO BE DIFFERENT

Recommended Books

Making A Place For Women: A Resource Handbook On Women And The Built Environment
Marjorie Bulos (ed), compiled by Jos Boys with Rosa Ainley and Maureen Farish,
The Women's Design Service.

Defining Design History And The History Of Design
Judy Altfield   Pluto Press   1989

Our Work, Our Lives, Our Words: Women's History And Women's Work
Leonore Davidoff and Belinda Westover (eds), MacMillan Education

Girls, Wives And Factory Lives
A Pollit   MacMillan   1981

Making Space: Women And The Man- Made Environment
Matrix   Pluto Press   1984

Women In Cities
J.Little et al (eds)   MacMillan   1988

Women And Social Policy: A Reader
Clare Ungerson (ed)   MacMillan   1985

Women, Human Settlements And Housing
Caroline Moser and Linda Peake (eds) Tavistock   1987

Brothers: Male Dominance And Technological Change
Cynthia Cockburn   Pluto Press   1983

Smothered By Invention: Technology In Women's Lives
W. Faulkner and E. Arnold   Pluto Press   1985

The Egalitarian City
Janet Boles (ed)   Praeger Press   1986

A Guide To The Health And Safety At Work Etc. Act 1974
Health and Safety Executive (HS(R)6)

Community Planning and Building
London Voluntary Service Council   1990
68 Chalton St, London NW11JR   £5.95 inc. P&P

Organisations

The Womens Environmental Network
287 City Road, London EC1 1LA   Tel 071 490 2511

Rights Of Women
52 - 54 Featherstone St, London EC1 8RT   Tel 071 251 6577

Women In Education
The National Association. PO Box 149 Preston Lancs. PR2 1HF

Womens Rights Unit, National Council For Civil Liberties
 21 Tabard St, London SE1 4LA   Tel 071 403 3888

Women In Manual Trades
52 - 54 Featherstone St, London EC1Y 8RT Tel 071 251 9192

Women In Construction Advisory Group
South Bank House, Black Prince Rd, London SE1 7SJ Tel 071 587 1802

Matrix Feminist Architectural Cooperative
The Print House 18 Ashwin St, London E8 3DL   Tel 071 249 7603

Health And Safety Executive
Belgrave House, Greyfriars, Northampton, NN1 2BS. Tel 0604 212333

City Centre: Information And Advice For Office Workers
32-35 Featherstone Street, London, EC1Y 8QX. Tel 071 608 1338

Women's Design Service
Information and Resources on Women and the Built Environment
18 Ashwin Street, London, E8 3DL.

Homeless Action - Housing for single women
52 - 54 Featherstone St, London EC1Y 8RT Tel 071 251 6783

Shelter
Room 201, 88 Old St, London EC1V 9HU Tel 071 253 0202

Women Prisoners Resource Centre
1 Thorpe Close, London W10 5XL   Tel   081 968 3121

Association Of Community Technical Aid Centres
Royal Institution Colquitt St Liverpool L1 4DE   Tel 051 708 7607

Equal Rights Dept. Trades Union Congress
Congress House, Gt. Russel St, London WC1B 3LS

National Homeworking Unit
Wolverly House, 18 Digbeth , Birmingham B5 6BJ Tel 021 643 6352

CHAPTER 10
DEALING WITH VIOLENCE OR ITS THREAT

This chapter is divided into two:

Defining self defence

Self defence when under threat

Some Definitions

Violence is one of the ugliest forms of human behaviour. It is a ruthless and forceful expression of power against another person or people. Hints of violence are displayed often however, without there being any physical contact. Growling, clenched fists, specific threats and excessive shouting are examples.

The threat of violence can be as powerful as the violence itself.

There appear to be three levels at which the violence-prone individual will operate. It is important to remember that ANY of us could become violent given the unique circumstances which may require it. It is also important to acknowledge that an action of self defence MAY be an extremely violent one.

THE THREE LEVELS OF VIOLENCE

AGGRESSION

A threatening or hostile behaviour which expects submission or subservience.

HARASSMENT

An extension of aggression which undermines, is often frightening and usually continues over a period of time.

VIOLENCE

The end result of aggression when total submission is expected.

Excessive verbal and emotional abuse can be seen to be violent, whilst physical injury or damage is clear violence.

Gaining Back Control

The reasons for this behaviour have been described in the Chapters Knowing Power and Knowing Our Fear. In this chapter we will consider how we can deal with unwarranted personal violence against us.

What's The Difference Between Physical Assertiveness And Self Defence?

When an individual becomes aggressive towards us they are expecting us to submit to them and their will. This in turn may make us feel aggressive or frightened in response.

There will then be a spiral reaction between the parties.

Answering these questions may help you discover who the true aggressor is:

1. Is the aggressor more powerful than me?

2. Am I more powerful than the aggressor?

3. Do I expect this other person to submit to me and if so why?

4. Does the aggressor expect me to submit to them?

If we conclude that the other person's aggression is completely unwarranted, and *is* threatening us - as a racial or sexual attack may be - we then have to move into ANOTHER FORM OF BEHAVIOUR.

This will be a SELF DEFENCE behaviour.

A self defence behaviour:

1. **Reacts** to the power of the aggressor

2. **Assesses** the power balance between both parties

3. **Decides** on which action is best for either:

   - survival

   - or fighting to disarm and disable

   - or fighting to win

However, the physically assertive woman may deal with aggression and even the threat of violence without necessarily having to use any self defence techniques. She may, after all not NEED them.

> **Because:**
>
> 1. She may not need to react to the aggressor because the aggressor has no real power.
>
> 2. She has *already* asessed the power situation and *knows* herself to be as powerful if not more.
>
> 3. Her survival is not being threatened and she is confident in her ability to disarm.

So, if a woman's personal power is such that she feels thoroughly in control and is endeavouring to bring back the control of the other person, she will not need to resort to self defence methods.

- The obvious scenario for this would be when an individual of lesser height and build threatens a woman who is physically assertive. She may not be *frightened* of the aggresssor because physical height and strength would win in the end.

  She can deal with the situation sensitively and with the use of personal power which also enables the other person to come back to 'sense'. We do this all the time with children and young people.

Usually, of course, women are of smaller build than men and therefore feel a particularly obvious disadvantage. Even so, the physically assertive woman remembers her capacity for emotional and physical strength and will use this knowledge to maintain an assertive stance with an aggressor. She still may not be frightened.

It is at the point of *real threat* that the physically assertive woman will allow alarm bells to ring and she would then take a

SELF DEFENCE MODE

What Is Self Defence Mode?

> **If we remember that self defence behaviour expects to:**
>
> *decide* on which action is best for either:
> > survival
> > or fighting to disarm and disable
> > or fighting to win
>
> We realise that this may include verbally or physically taking action.
>
> **So, defending ourselves may mean:**
>
> - doing anything which allows us to survive
> - or fighting back with words or physical action with the intention of disarming or disabling
> - or fighting to win back whatever it was we felt we were going to lose

Your need for self defence mode may come at a very EARLY stage or LATER as the aggressor's actions become more apparent.

It is essential to understand that the use of a physical self defence technique against another person is also an action of violence. There will be an intention to disable physically the aggressor so that escape or complete disarming may occur. Believing in our capacity for this violence can protect us through very difficult and sometimes life-threatening situations.

Sometimes the use of violence against an aggressor will actually mean the difference between saving ourselves and horrible injury or death. We need feel no guilt or question about that action. What we do have to analyse is when and how it is best used - to benefit us.

Self defence in Britain seems to grow in theory all the time. As more and more women give their contribution to the sharing of experience and ability we are learning that self defence, in its *broadest sense,* can and does, accommodate just about all forms of emotional and physical self protection.

This unearthing of ancient protection mechanisms gives us the ability to *survive* better.

> **But, is it only survival that we want?**

There is no question that we live in a violent and exploitative world. However, building our personal power base as assertive women allows us the opportunity to live our lives without fear.

Is it right that we should expect to have to live subjected to the potential threat and violence of oppressors and aggresssors always? It seems that the self defence movement may unwittingly take us up the street where we expect to exist *constantly* only in *response* to male or racist or homophobic violence.

> **In other words:**
>
> **We live in fear because we are aware of the potential of threat. So, we end up *reacting* to potential aggressors even when they do not threaten us. We expect them to be powerful.**

This can then make us victims even when we don't want it to.

It is also an inaccurate theory of the way life really is, anyway .... *we* can be as violent as any man.

- For instance

    Certain racist women use violence against black women, without hesitation. As do some ruling class women against those they have power over.

> **The alternative for the physically and emotionally assertive woman is:**
>
> that she assumes that she WILL NOT be attacked, first. (She feels comfortable in the knowledge of her own strength and is prepared to exhibit it so that potential aggressors have already recognised HER power.)
>
> *Then*, when alarm bells start sounding because there is danger - a threat is apparent - she will go into SELF DEFENCE MODE.
>
> She leaves behind her life without fear and acknowledges that she is *registering fear*.
>
> Because she is knowledgeable of what makes her frightened she then decides HOW to react to her fear.
>
> She will endeavour to respond to her fear constructively.

This way of life depends on a woman being very aware and open about the nature of her surroundings, environment and relationships. She allows her protective intuition to play a very strong part in her life.

Whereas, living in self defence mode persistently forces us to be always frightened and alert.

Until we recognise and own our power AND our ability to defend ourselves we exist in a secondary role to the oppressor. We have already conceded to the oppressor his or her power if we are expecting, relentlessly, to have to defend ourselves.

> **The assumption of no-attack is not a naive and childish expectation.**
>
> **It is the expression of *comfortable strength*.**

It is living your life in a dangerous world, having gained skill and powers in handling the threats that may arise.

The difference between physical assertiveness and self defence behaviour is that it allows us to relax into our own personhood first. If a threat then arises and we are frightened, we may legitimately take out our 'monster' apparel and become really as aggressive and even as violent as the situation may call for.

Without a distinction between the two we blur when we are being aggressive for necessity and when we may actually be able to deal with a threat without resorting to counter-attack.

The Difference Between The Oppressor And The Oppressed.

The oppressor lives their life comfortably in the knowledge that society at large and institutions will protect their personal interests and therefore their aggressive behaviour.

They may well have no assumption that the oppressed will turn around and attack them. They might not live in fear of attack. **They have comfortable power.**

The oppressed do have to live under the threats of the oppressor. As always the victims have to take certain responsibility for the situation. Rising above the threats of male violence and finding our own ways to become powerful gives us the opportunity to have comfortable strength.

> When comfortable strength meets comfortable power the one who succeeds will be she who comprehends all the influences in the interaction.
>
> It will be she who has knowledge of many sources of strength and she who knows how to use them with dignity and control.

Comfortable Strength Is A Physically Assertive Woman.

- The physically assertive woman knows her own personal powers, she knows her own fears and the level to which they motivate her. She knows how physically strong she is and how her posture affects her messages and bearing.

  She will be in touch with her inner self - her intuition and her own style of dealing with difficulty. She is aware of her environment and above all else she has a relationship with the resources around her and accepts her responsibilty in using them.

Many women's self defence classes teach these qualities.

> But, it seems important not to confuse these skills with self defence techniques.

Being in touch with our intuition and inner strength need not have anything at all to do with violence or aggression. It may as easily be used to be productive and creative. Receiving telepathic messages from a friend may urge you to do something very useful for both of you. It's part of a whole way of life.

Judith Lowe, Self Defence Coordinator to the ILEA until 1990 clearly makes this point in her paper in Appendix II. Her progressive leadership and teacher training of self defence teachers in London provides a rationale to grow continuously and develop as whole human beings.

We cannot, in this chapter, consider all the self defence techniques available to us. There are books written which do far greater justice than can be attempted here.

The book "Her Wits About Her" also demonstrates vivid examples of how women have fought back and won. All those stories display the wide and exhilarating variety of methods women use to not be defeated. (18)

What follows therefore is description and definition of some simple methods of physical self defence techniques. The reader is urged to attend a women's self defence class to become familiar and experienced in using them.

Figure 36

PHYSICAL SELF DEFENCE TECHNIQUES - SELF DEFENCE MODE

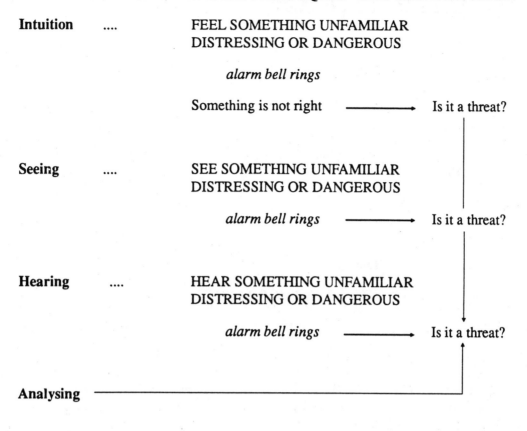

Intuition .... FEEL SOMETHING UNFAMILIAR
DISTRESSING OR DANGEROUS

alarm bell rings

Something is not right ⟶ Is it a threat?

Seeing .... SEE SOMETHING UNFAMILIAR
DISTRESSING OR DANGEROUS

alarm bell rings ⟶ Is it a threat?

Hearing .... HEAR SOMETHING UNFAMILIAR
DISTRESSING OR DANGEROUS

alarm bell rings ⟶ Is it a threat?

Analysing

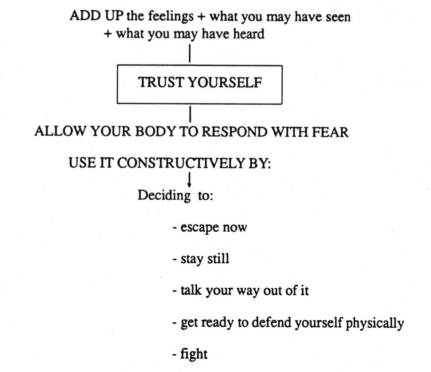

ADD UP the feelings + what you may have seen
+ what you may have heard

TRUST YOURSELF

ALLOW YOUR BODY TO RESPOND WITH FEAR

USE IT CONSTRUCTIVELY BY:

Deciding to:

- escape now

- stay still

- talk your way out of it

- get ready to defend yourself physically

- fight

When Under Threat

You have decided that there is a real threat and you are now in self defence mode.

The body will take over part of your reactions.

You will be urged by the adrenalin to either:

panic

escape

break away

stay still

talk

get ready to fight or

fight

TRUSTING YOURSELF is the first important part of defending yourself. It means that your body reaction initially may well be more knowing and definite than your analysis.

Your physical reaction tells you something and will nearly always give you an opportunity to *work with it*. Allowing your body to defend you puts your whole being into action. The aggressor then has to cope with your physical strength as well as your analysis.

Following are broad outlines of techniques which may be used as a result of your physical reactions:

Panic

This will make it feel as if everything is out of control. We are very vulnerable when panicking.

However, the elements to rely on when panicking are:

a. Panic is an obvious reminder of HIGH ENERGY levels.

b. This could allow you to consider yourself as FIRE. It could prompt you to think speed, agility, flickering and uncontrollable flames.

c. This might then give the opportunity to relate the two qualities of fire to your situation:
    - uncatchable
    - totally destructive

d. Panic may then become a central and unquenchable desire for action which may not only save your life or save you from injury but also regains your position of power.

e. It is best to MOVE ON from panic however, at the earliest possible moment because it is usually always better to draw analysis to your defence. This will then become a calming influence.

f. If you have the sort of personality which easily panics, your own self defence training may be best organised around understanding your reactions in ordinary circumstances as a means of preparation.

g. Panicking about panicking doesn't help too much. Allow yourself to feel fear and use it.

Gaining Back Control

Escape Now

The threat is apparent and you decide escape is the best form of self defence. It may also be the safest.

Points to remember:

a.   Your body will give you enough energy to escape as fast as you can with the methods best suited for you. A wheelchair user will balance up whether escape is the best idea for her with other alternatives, like using break away techniques.

     If speed is not a choice for you in escaping - remember that the body is geared up for speed even if you can't take advantage of it. Use that energy in other ways.

b.   You might think of yourself as WATER - something which moves easily in response to the pull of gravity. When escaping become fluid and blending. The attacker can't catch you and even if you were caught, your body can react like water in the hand.

     Conversely, a wheelchair user may decide to become more HEAVY and well grounded into the chair. An immovable force can prove to an attacker that you are no easy game.

c.   You may not want to escape with speed. Sometimes a quiet withdrawal, a 'slipping silently past', a 'becoming invisible' may be equally helpful.

d.   Escaping succesfully allows you to tell the tale later. Many of us use this technique all the time without thinking about it. It seems to be of no note because 'nothing happened' you were only relying on 'gut feeling'.

Sometimes analysing why, when and how you escape from situations will let you see the nature of power relationships in your life more clearly. Where there is a dominant and domineering relationship there will always be a threat of violence under the surface.

Your escape reactions may give you more information about the form of threats, than was first acknowledged.

Break Away Techniques

Broadly, these fall into 5 categories:

evading

   pulling out

      pushing away

         moving with the force and

            startling

Evading

For example:

- Maintain your balance

- Keep grounded as if into the EARTH

- When moving be aware of your need for posture and lowering your centre of gravity

- Keep movements unpredictable but concise

- AIR is invisible and yet may be volatile like the wind. Behaving like the air may allow you to move from heaviness to becoming light. The wheelchair user may portray this lightness with her upper body. Then, if an attacker tries to hold or grab s/he may be very surprised to find a forceful heaviness in the lower body.

Pulling out

For examples see figures 37 to 46 on the next pages:

All the following diagrams have been reproduced from the book "Streetwise" (19) with kind permission of the authors, Judith Lowe and Isabel Wright.

Pulling out

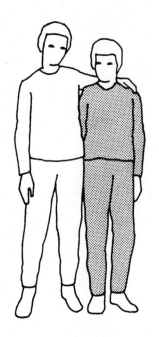

Fig. 37

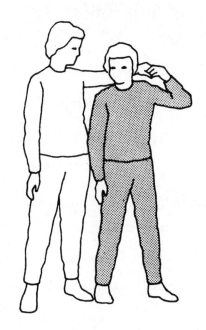

Fig. 38

Pick the attacker's hand off your shoulder

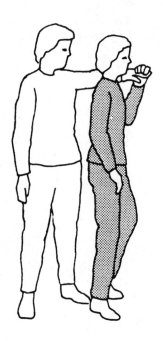

Fig. 39

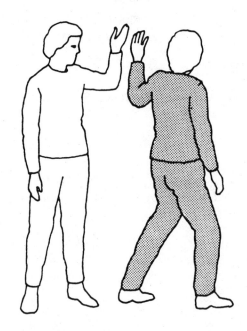

Fig. 40

Turn around and walk **OUT** and **AWAY**

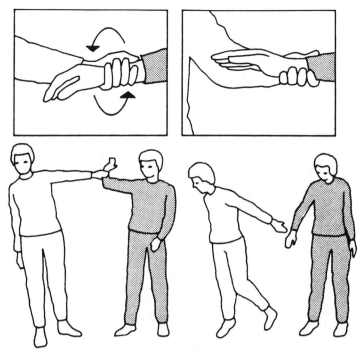

Figure 41
The attacker has grabbed your wrist. Their grip is weakest in the gap between the thumbs and index finger.

Figure 42
Twist your wrist towards their gap and pull out of the hold.

Pushing away

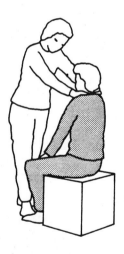

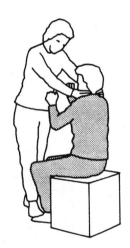

Figures 43
A wheelchair user will benefit from this technique. The attacker puts their hands around your throat. Lean back slightly to relieve the pressure on your wind pipe.

Figure 44
Clench your fists and bring your arms up between the attacker's.

Gaining Back Control

Pushing away continued.

Figure 45
Push your forearms strongly against the inside of their arms.

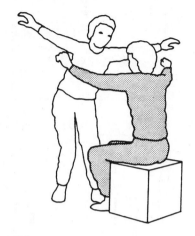

Figure 46
Force their arms apart as powerfuly as you can.

Moving with the force

For example:

- Being grabbed by the hair: Go *towards* the hand holding the hair - thus taking away the pain.

- When being lunged at: use their lack of balance to allow their momentum towards you to make them fall.

Startling

For example:

- Using your voice: to shout, make noise, give clear messages, to be unpredictable

- Using anti-social behaviour: pick your nose, blubber, become like a monster

- Using your understanding: doing or saying something that might undermine the attacker

- Using the resources around you: flinging, threatening, noise, cover, as extensions of you and your environment.

The above techniques have referred to the four elements FIRE, WATER, EARTH AND AIR. They are commonly used in preparation for self defence techniques (made popular for women by Kaleghl Quinn) and may be defined in the ways best suited to individual women. The above ideas are merely examples of visualising and believing in forces far greater than ourselves. (20)

We are familiar with these elements already since the Chapter Earth, Wind, Fire and Water describes their NATURAL Force.

Their use prompts us to imagine new ways of dealing with situations. For those with some lack of mobility or painful mobility these elements can enhance those parts of your body which you are able to move. They can also give meaning to those parts which you cannot move.

- Pain could be like fire.

  Paralysed legs could be part of the earth.

  The absence of a limb may draw attention to air.

  The blood stream gives energy to your whole body and moves like water.

Stay Still

> **Staying still may happen in response to threat because of:**
>
> - numbness
> - being physically unable to move
> - consciously deciding to

It is still another very valuable reaction to the threat you are experiencing. It is a normal function of adrenalin and can be life-saving.

Numbness

This is a clear shock reaction and part of feeling distressed. It can be very powerful if your initial body reaction understands the situation more than your thinking does.

Perhaps sudden movement or any gesture would further aggravate the attacker. It allows you time to recover, make decisions and feel your body energy and power.

> **The characteristics of numbness are such that they might 'transport' you away from the scene. This is a normal reaction when we experience an extreme trauma. Some women have said they could see the whole scene as *if they weren't part of it.***

This may reduce the dreadful horror and pain incurred, rather like an anaesthetic. It may actually be the *only* solution if there is no choice other than to submit. This therefore may be true for children who suffer at the hands of adults.

Forgetting is also part of the numbness reaction. If we are subject to repeated attack it may be the only source of surviving it - to forget it. During crisis and attack this is really beneficial. It can become problematic later though. There is especially a need to understand those fears which spring from real and dreadful past experience if, for instance, we have been traumatised during childhood.

Being numb is as it suggests. We don't feel as we might normally. Often we are not conscious of it until after the event. It closes off the body from the mind. It is also known as 'freezing'.

Gaining Back Control

This description draws attention to the immobilising effect of becoming numb. It is the opposite of panicking. Everything becomes deadened.

> **However, it becomes an advantage when you realise that your mind may be working ten to the dozen trying to take it all in.**

Remember, the attacker will have planned the attack in some way or other - they will have made a decision to do it. Sometimes they plan days in advance. You have to catch up with that in a matter of seconds. Let yourself register that your body is still caring for you by immobilising you. It is giving you a chance to STOP.

Being physically unable to move.

This may occur because you are pinned to the floor, wall or to the attacker or you may be imprisoned in some way.

You may be immobilised because of a personal physical disability. This might be the most terrifying part of any attack. It possibly precedes even worse to come. You MAY decide that you will incur less damage by NOT fighting. You may decide to stay still to save your life.

Here trusting yourself is so very, very important. Your body will tell you if you have any chances in fighting and winning. Hear it, feel it and remain vigilant for any opportunity which may display a weakness or vulnerability in the attacker. Possibly the attacker will not expect a movement from you if you have not struggled. You then have the element of surprise as a powerful weapon against her/him.

Consciously deciding to stay still.

You will notice from the above that emphasis has been placed on allowing the numbness reaction to give you time to think. Actually, deciding to stay still IS a powerful option. It is even more so if you are able to remind yourself of a calming technique like for instance, visualising something which gives you confidence or consciously breathing correctly.

It will precede a thought out strategy for defending yourself.

Surprisingly, there are usually more seconds available to us than we might imagine during the course of an attack.

Talking Your Way Out Of It

There may be many good reasons to do this. Most of us use this to defuse all sorts of potentially violent situations.

> **Following the step by step guide:**
>   feel intuition
>   see danger
>   hear danger
>   analyse
>
> STOP, LOOK AND LISTEN

This gives a good start to the methods you use to defend yourself.

You have a vast armoury of words, wisdoms and insight to rely on, especially if, as is usually the case, you know the attacker. Use a tone of voice which best suits the occasion. Don't be afraid to change your tone if it's necessary - to a softer or stronger one for instance.

Do try to think through the consequences of what you say. You don't need a more angry attacker!

Get Ready To Defend Yourself Physically

If you decide to attack the aggressor it is always best to ascertain the situation first.

'If I attack will I win?'

'Do I know what I will do and where?'

'How much do I remember about self defence?'

A blind rage of attack is what the aggressor may expect from you (and is associated with the 'hysterical woman' idea) beating on his chest and all....

Stopping still to think it out lets you weigh up the situation.

"If I attack will I win? "
- you need to BELIEVE that you will.

"Do I know what I will do and where?"
- this depends on remembering what are the attacker's vulnerable areas, what are your weapons and if you can follow through one action with another.

Vulnerable Areas

Figure 47

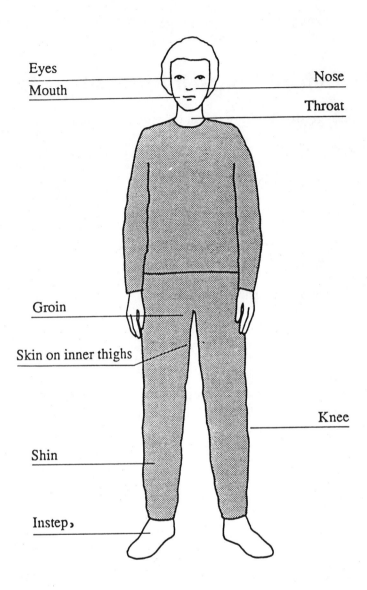

Eyes
Mouth
Nose
Throat
Groin
Skin on inner thighs
Knee
Shin
Instep

Your weapons

Most parts of the body that you can move will be a potential weapon. However, it is best to know HOW to use your weapons to maximise the effect and to minimise damaging yourself.

The hands

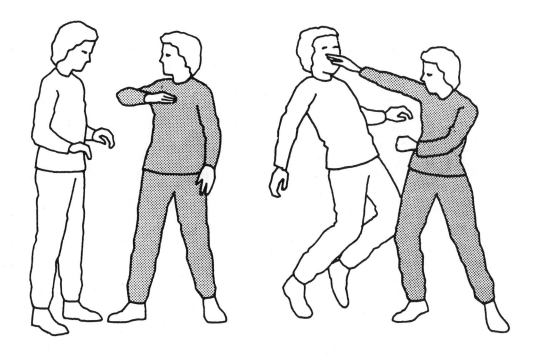

Figures 48 & 49.

A strike with the knife edge part of the hand underneath the attacker's nose.

Your weapons

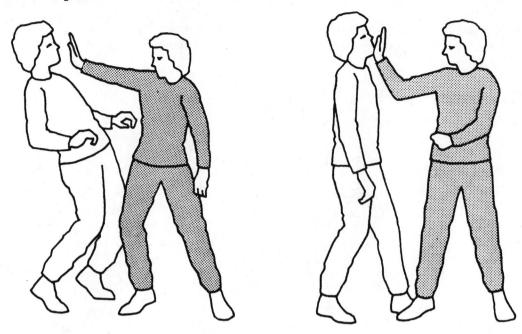

Figures 50 & 51

A strike with the heel of the hand underneath the attacker's chin.

Figure 52

A poke to the eye, keeping the fingers stiff.

Your weapons

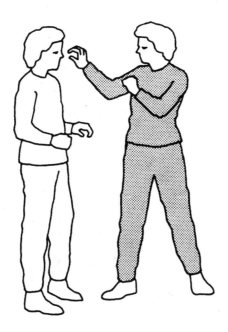

Figure 53

A claw to the face - the attacker's cheeks would be scratched.

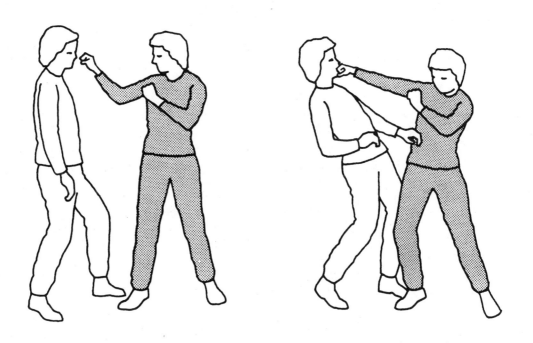

Figures 54 & 55

Punch to the attacker's nose - remember to keep the fists straight.

Your weapons

Figures 56 & 57

Knuckle to the eye - make a fist with the first joint of the middle finger protruding.

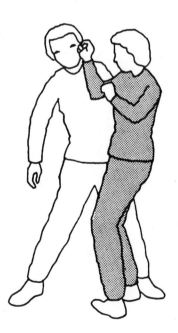

Figure 58

A hammer blow with the side of the fist to the temple.

Grab, twist and pull

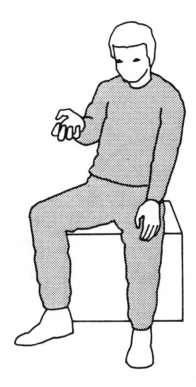

Figure 59

This is a useful technique in whatever position we are in but can be particularly helpful for wheelchair users.

This figure shows the defender preparing to grab, twist and pull the attacker's testicles. This technique may be applied to any soft, fleshy parts of the body ie, inside of the leg, the ears, nose, lips or little fingers. Twisting ensures pain!

Use both hands

Like clapping them with vigour and cupped hands at both ears.

The elbow

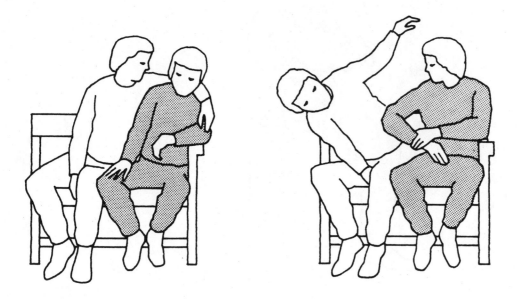

Figures 60 & 61

You can use your elbow for instance, by taking your wrist and thrusting your elbow
backwards sharply, into the attacker's ribs or stomach. This can be done standing as well.

The head

Head-butting is best done with extreme caution but may be a technique available for wheel
chair users especially if you have hold of the attacker's ears as well.

The knee

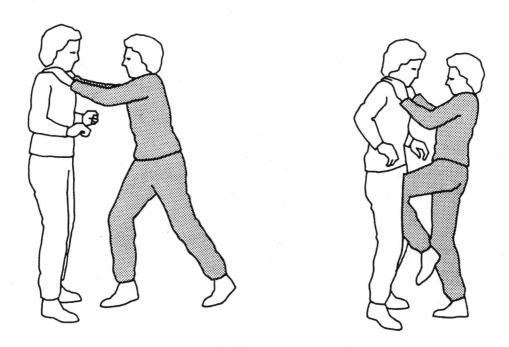

Figures 62 & 63

Knee to the groin - support yourself by holding on to the attacker. Bring the knee up sharply, well between the legs.

Gaining Back Control

Trunk and legs

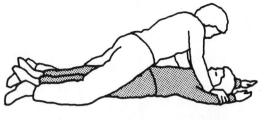

Figure 64
The attacker is lying on top of you, holding your arms down.

Figure 65
Bend either knee up between their legs

Figure 66
Firmly place the sole of your foot flat on the floor.

Figure 67
Keeping your foot firmly planted, push your hip on the side of the bent knee into the attacker. At the same time bring your hands down by your side to upset your attacker's balance.

Figure 68
Roll over powerfully to throw your attacker off you. Your hips act as both a strong lever and support.

Figure 69
Escape as quickly as possible.

The feet

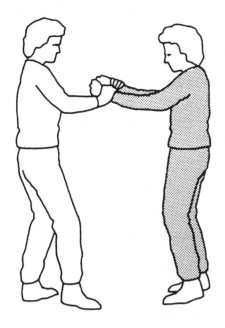

Figure 70
An attacker has grabbed your wrists

Figure 71
Use their hold to balance yourself

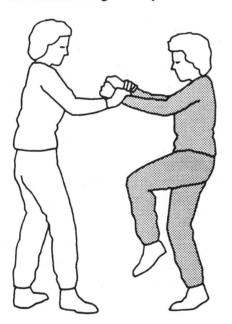

Figure 72
Now kick to the shins - be careful if you have soft footware on.

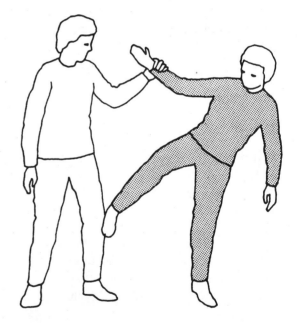

Figure 73
Alternatively, use the attacker's hold to give you balance. A sideways kick to the attacker's knee uses the side of your foot to make the strike.

You can also use your feet to stamp on the aggressor's foot.

Gaining Back Control

Follow through

To follow through is to think 'secondary action'.

It takes your self defence strategy seriously by reminding you that it's no good whacking hard a vulnerable area and then not knowing what to do.

It means that you have got another action ready to *gain a second advantage* against the aggressor.

The follow-through could come in any combination:

- Hit and escape

- Escape and sound an alarm

- Hit and hit again

- Hit and hold

- Hold and sound an alarm

- Break-away then hit

- Break-away then hold

Penny Gulliver who is Australian, calls some follow-throughs "turning the tap on, turning the tap off". In other words finishing off the job. (21) Learning self defence with this in mind both challenges us to 'go the whole way' and builds confidence. You might just carry on turning the tap on and off with as many techniques as you have available to you.

Some more fighting techniques follow.

Fight

Women's self defence techniques are a mix between the strictest knowledge of martial arts methods and 'dirty' tactics of street fighting. Sticking your fingers into someone's eyes, gauging your nails down the side of a face is pure, unadulterated violence and it may save your life.

Women's self defence teaches that it is alright to behave like this when under physical attack. In a way it's merely catching up with the boys who had the benefit of tumbling, boxing, wrestling and fighting with mates as they grew up. We should have the confidence to use such tactics if we are compelled to.

Earlier we considered how to use our body weapons against an attacker. Now we have decided that our best course of action is to fight.

Here are some guidelines:

1. You must want to win.

2. You will have to be ruthless.

3. You are equipped with body and mental facilities to fight.

4. You are mindful of continuing to defend yourself.

5. You stop fighting when you have won.

6. You are aware that as 'victor' you may have to answer to the authorities for the damage you inflicted.

7. Once you have won you recognise your power and temper it.

There is a need to continue to defend yourself when fighting and one method is to 'block' or deflect blows. The other is to put the aggressor into a hold which is both painful and debilitating.

Blocking

Blocking deflects the attacks of the aggressor. It stops an intended blow from striking a vulnerable area of your body by taking the blow with another part - like the forearm. The idea is to protect your centre line by lowering the body into the grounded position. Then raising the arm to push away the attacks.

It works on the same principles as a sword fight. However, a balanced defend-attack situation is to deflect with one arm whilst spontaneously engaging the other fist and using it in an attack. That is a classical follow-through situation.

Sometimes deflecting can also turn into an attack, like the pushing aside of a leg coming up to kick you. This would then unbalance the attacker. Guarding your face with the other hand and fore-arm then prevents a further attack to one of your vulnerable areas.

Defend - attack is the usual momentum of a fight. Watching the men fighting on TV - boxing, judo, karate and wrestling will give lots of evidence of how attack-defend momentum builds up.

Blocking

A   B   A   B

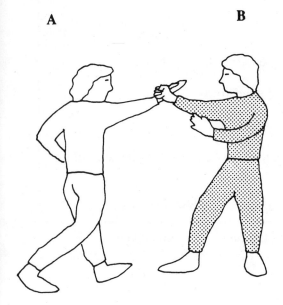

Figure 74

A blocks B's straight punch with A's wrist. Notice that B's left hand keeps guard while the right goes into attack.

Figure 75

A immediately follows through with a front kick, but B deflects this by twisting her arm over and sweeping it away to her right. She continues to guard her face.

Adapted from 'Self Defence for Women', by Diana Warren-Holland, Denise Russell-Jones and Rachel Stewart, Hamlyn (22)

Holds

Putting an opponent into a hold often depends on speed and surprise. It also depends on the opponent not knowing how to get out of the hold.

An attacker may well consider you truly defeated if they have got their arm around your neck. However, twisting your head to the side away from the crook of the attacker's arm allows you to breath and then to attack with a punch from your elbow into the solar plexus.

The kind of holds useful to you are those which turn the aggressor's attack into something which benefits you.

Figures 37 to 74 and Figures 76 to 79 have been reproduced from the book "Streetwise" by Judith Lowe and Isabel Wright, published by Ariel Books but sadly now out of print. However, your local library may have a copy of it.

Holds

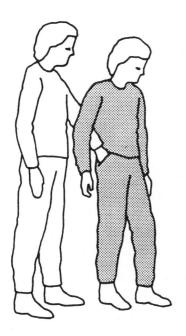

Figure 76
If you feel a thief's hand in your pocket

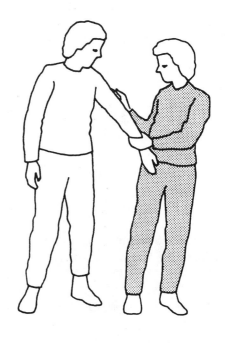

Figure 77
Grab their wrist firmly with one hand

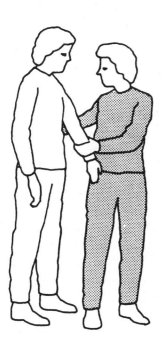

Figure 78
Push your other hand hard into the back of
their elbow

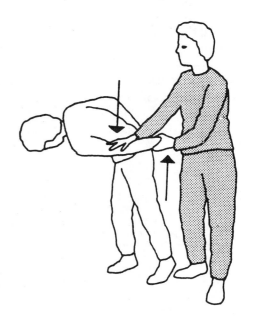

Figure 79
Pull their wrist up, pushing their elbow
down and force them away from you.

A hold relies on a locking mechanism between your body and the aggressor's. Restraining someone in a sturdy lock puts you into a very strong position BUT never expect it to be held without thorough concentration.

If you can call for assistance or follow through with another attack do it!

Use the advantage to finish off the job properly!

Martial Arts

Martial arts are ancient forms of self defence, mostly oriental in origin. "Self Defence for Women" has an excellent chapter describing the differences between the styles. (22) It also succinctly points out that a number of the arts were developed by women. The Wing Chun style of Kung Fu was devised by Wing Chun herself - she was initially taught by a nun!

The wives of the Samurai fought with long bladed spears to defend their homes and it is now known as the Naginata martial art.

In the strictest sense martial arts will be taught as a discipline following time tested and true techniques. They mostly rely on principles which understand the exercise of power, in their methods.

Taekwon-do holds these five basic tenets: courtesy, integrity, perseverance, self control and indomitable spirit.

Many women have discovered the vast benefits both physically and mentally of studying a martial art. It is liberating to learn that we may exercise power through agility, flexibility, speed, stamina, coordination and balance.

> **Turning the attacker's size and height into an advantage for you seems extraordinary and yet is the basis of most martial arts.**

Women are urged to take up training in a martial art. It can provide a long term challenge which channels and focuses the physical power we all have. It is worth searching for one that suits yourself. Though this may seem impossible in so many male dominated clubs, it's important to make a noise and demand that clubs and sports centres provide adequate services for women.

Recommended Reading And Video

Self Defence For Women
Penny Gulliver Video Seven Dimensions 18 Armstrong St Middle Park Victoria 3206 Australia

Self Defence For Women
Diana Warren-Holland. Denise Russell-Jones. Rachel Stewart Hamlyn 1987

Her Wits About Her: Self-defence Success Stories By Women
Denise Caignon and Gail Groves, eds The Women's Press,   1989
- This book lists many useful local resources and addresses on self-defence

Women In The Martial Arts: A New Spirit Rising
Linda Atkinson   Dodd, Mead and Co.   1983

The Hidden Struggle
 - Statutory and Voluntary Response to Violence Against Black Women in the Home
Amina Mama   Runnymede Trust   1989

Stopping Rape: Successful Survival Strategies
Pauline Bart, Patricia O'Brien   Pergamon Press   1985

Fear Into Anger: A Manual Of Self-defense For Women
Py Bateman   Nelson-Hall Inc.   1978

Fight Back! Feminist Resistance To Male Violence
Frederique Delacoste and Felice Newman (eds) Cleis Press   1981

Every Woman's Guide To Self Defence
Kathleen Hudson   St. Martin's Press   1978

Stand Your Ground: A Woman's Guide To Self-preservation
Kaleghl Quinn Macdonald   Optima   1988

The Woman's Guide To Staying Safe
Cheryl Reimold   Cloverdale Press/Monarch Press   1985

In Defence Of Ourselves: A Rape Prevention Handbook For Women
Linda Sanford,Tschirhart and Fetter   N.J.Doubleday   1979

Attitude: Commonsense Defense For Women
Lisa Sliwa   Crown Publishers   1986

Fear Or Freedom: A Woman's Options In Social Survival And Physical Defence
Susan Smith   Mother Courage Press   1986

Getting Free: A Handbook For Women In Abusive Relationships
Ginny NiCarthy   Seal Press   1986

Organisations

Asha Womens Resource Centre
27 Santley St, London SW4 7QF Tel 071 274 8854

Shakti Womens Aid
12 Picardy Place, Edinburgh EH1 3GT Tel 031 557 4010

Welsh Womens Aid
38 - 48 Crwys Rd, Cardiff CF2 4NN Tel 0222 390874

Womens Aid Feeration
PO Box 391, Bristol BS99 7WS Tel 0272 428368

Women Against Sexual Harasssment
242 Pentonville Rd, Kings Cross, London N1 9UN Tel 071 833 0222

Black Womens Campaign Against Rape And Sexual Abuse
c/o 241 Albion Rd London N16 9JT

Criminal Injuries Compensation Board
Whitington House, 19 - 30 Alfred Place, Chenies St, London WC1E 7LG Tel 071 636 2812

Rape Crisis Centres
Tel 071 837 1600

CHAPTER 11
BECOMING ABLE

This chapter is best read in association with the Chapter Managing Stress, which highlights methods of releasing ourselves.

We explore:

A definition of becoming able

    Our damage

        Our pain

            Our healing

                Our learning to become more able

Becoming Able Defined

Dependency

We are too often placed in a position of dependency on other more powerful people.

If, as a woman, we have been taught to rely on a man for income or protection, status or wisdom, then we have stopped our own abilities to be independent in these areas. If we feel confident that we can live without the financial support of a man, we are in a stronger place to decide that we may want to be dependent, for whatever reason.

> **Those of us who have never had the support of a man will know how hard it is to be independent, and yet how much stronger we are.**

Conversely, an elderly man whose wife dies and who is unable to cook his own food, ends up again helpless and dependent on others to cook for him.

The way out of course is to learn HOW to become more independent. If we have been dependent on a man or men for 'protection' then we have to teach ourselves independence. We may start the process with learning self defence.

> **By its nature, independence gives us opportunities to learn and test out new abilities.**

The other way of looking at this is to suggest that when we become independent we can become more able. We are then in a far better position to CHOOSE when we wish to be dependent.

There are stages that we can go through to challenge ourselves in becoming more able in a world which constantly belittles the talents and strength of women or anyone else who does not fit into the stereotypes promoted by ruling interests.

Becoming Able

First:

we have to see ourselves in the way WE WANT TO. That is, we cannot let other people's power over us define what we want to think about ourselves.

Second:

we do all depend on one another - it is part of life and of community living.

However, we have to *choose* what is important for us as individuals to be independent in. It will usually be a priority because we cannot do and know about everything.

It is no coincidence though, that so few women have been taught practical skills at school (apart from homemaking).

So, if we have never been taught how to use spanners, get greasy and mend the car, we are still dependent on someone else to repair it. The likelihood is it will be a man.

Even so, a surge of interest by women over the last decade has resulted in MANY women BECOMING MORE ABLE in Do-It-Yourself activities.

Better designed tools, more books and explanatory leaflets, more accessible DIY stores have all contributed to women deciding to do the job themselves.

Third:

once we start to realise how dependent and ill-equipped we are we start then to see how disabled we are or have become in so many other areas of life.

Fourth:

we then have to make further decisions about the LEVEL at which we wish to operate.

This can only be done after we have really understood the tension between:

What we could do (realistically) :	**What limits we have physically and emotionally**

Our Level Of Ability

We may be intellectually disabled if we are told as children that we are thick and stupid. We are also likely to believe it. Sometimes it takes a lifetime's struggle to 'become able' to overcome that early damage, to believe that actually we are intelligent.

We may be emotionally disabled all the time by others who want to keep us down and stifle our feelings.

We may be physically disabled by our never being taught or shown how to use tools, machines or engines correctly.

> **But, it is still an emotional decision on our part to believe we _can't use_ machines or tools.**

It is argued in this chapter that realistically we _might_ be able to do anything _so long as_ we have the right information, tools and understanding of what could happen.

Our dilemma continues however, to be that of balancing what is naturally available to us, with what we need to achieve a task.

- We will not be able to drive if we have no car. A safe road also helps. If we have a car, a safe road and have been taught the correct skills, we have the opportunity to drive ourselves.

  But, we lose the opportunity again if we have no arms.

  Even so. If it were a priority for us, and others also agreed, a car can be invented which can use leg control rather than arms. People are using cars already with these adjustments.

> **ALL inventions start with either a need or a desire. Put both together and invention is bound to follow.**

In becoming able we have to understand our personal and physical power, in relation to our fear (perhaps even of achievement). We need then to understand how much stress we can ask our bodies and minds to respond to. If we are assertive we can use our environment around us to make us more comfortable and safe.

> **We do need each other to reach personal goals.**

Providing a means for others to become more able must by definition, undermine the ability of those who rule to assume powers which are not rightly theirs.

Being 'Able-bodied'

> **Who can indicate that they have no disabilities?**

To segregate those who are prepared to acknowledge, or are forced to acknowledge, that they have certain disabilities from others who arrogantly assume themselves to have none, is to make some people again 'less than' others.

Somehow, the people believing themselves to be 'able-bodied' carry with them assumptions that their disablities don't show, or do not damage other people.

> **An emotional disability can restrict an individual as successfully as a physical one.**

In this world it is unfortunate that speed, aggression, take-over and greed are values supported and sustained by those who generate them.

If we do not subscribe to these values we are *disadvantaged* but are we disabled?

We know that there are many other assets in life which will sustain us and assist us in enduring.

It is the allocation of physical resources which help us overcome physical disablity.

> **Is it TOO obvious to say that those thinking themselves to be 'able-bodied' restrict this allocation?**

Some of us may view self-seeking men and women as operating from a background of some personal disabling. WHY do SOME people HAVE TO BE *SO* rich and *SO* powerful? WHAT are they trying to protect themselves from? Perhaps maintaining personal power IS disabling?

The problem is of course that those under the influence of the personal power of others are often forcibly disabled by them. We do live in a thoroughly disabling society.

> **Calling ourselves 'able-bodied' is to assume that we have greater abilities to cope with either the physical or emotional world than those with disabilities.**
>
> **Have we?**

So What Is Disability?

We are disabled if we can't do something which allows us to be independent human beings. (It is important to add; and which does not impinge on the independence of others.)

For us to be really personally challenged about the nature of our disability we need to delve deep and face the unbearable.

Acknowledging disability, in the first instance, is one of the most painful of our experiences. It is no wonder we steer away from doing it. However, we cannot move on unless we know what it is that is disabling us.

Our Damage

We have all been damaged.

Somewhere along the way we will have been deeply hurt. It is impossible to live this life without some injury. We may have been physically damaged or emotionally damaged, or it may have been both. It is true that it appears that some people seem to escape injury more easily than others.

> **It is not coincidental that those with more physical privileges are likely to be less physically damaged.**

Even so, a man may look back at his life and find little on the surface to indicate any injury against him.

And yet, there will be. His being restricted in showing and sharing emotions and feelings, because he is a man, will have hurt him. He has a choice. Either he continues to show and share emotions and be penalised by other men who may label him as silly, soppy or sissy. Or, he may hide his real feelings - maybe put them away forever.

That damage then comes out in too many distortions and will be ready to damage other people around him. He has to work hard to overcome such encumberance.

> **Our damage is long and extensive.**

Our physical damage may have been with us since birth. Or it may have been inflicted along the way. Poor health care, or preventative care is the cause of far too much unnecessary injury.

Our emotional damage may be shrouded in its history, sometimes long forgotten, but it will still be there gnawing away at us.

Physical and emotional damage must be the greatest horror to bear.

- The girl who is raped, and maybe over long periods, by a male in her family, will suffer such damage that she may be injured for life.

  Many women walk now, having obliterated this terrible childhood torture because it would be too awful to understand the implications.

  Still however, the damage will motivate the woman.

  The excessive negation. The fear of ever really being able to trust. The expectation that it may happen again (it doesn't have to be the same way) can all conspire to disable her in such a manner that she may become frozen and be unable to reach out either for help or changing herself.

All of us react differently to injury. Some of us are able to take hurt in our stride and keep moving on. It is unusual though to not have scars lingering or wounds still festering.

Our Pain

It is important therefore, to acknowledge our damage, whatever it is.

If we can say, 'I have been damaged', we allow ourselves the opportunity to do something about the effects of that damage. If we deny the damage as if it was of no consequence we do not allow the opportunity to change and manage the effects of the injury.

If we can say, 'I have been hurt', we can participate with the real feelings we have and let them run their course.

> **Those feelings will change if we believe in our own personal desire to move on. They will change once you have let yourself say, 'Now I have had enough I want to move on.'**

It is a terrifying idea sometimes to think about the immensity of our emotions when we acknowledge our injury.

> **Our pain is as enormous as the feelings that go with it.**

It could seem as if it is thoroughly evil. As if it could totally dictate how we live. But, that is where we are at times. It CAN dictate to us. It DOES appear to be completely destructive. It CAN control us.

Our pain is essential to our survival.

It teaches us what we do and don't want out of this life.

It can turn against us so easily that we may become masochistic and invite it, because how could we live without it?

Physical pain disables and distorts our lives. It can be pure living hell.

But, we must acknowledge it.

THEN we can make choices.

● We can scream at the world 'I AM IN PAIN' and draw the world's attention to it - maybe then they'll hear?

We can ask/demand pain killers.

We can seek spiritual help.

We can keep looking for the right medical attention.

We might have to say 'Now I have to live with this'.

Whatever methods we have of resolving pain, believing it to be real is a recognition of your own self worth.

> **That you are worthy of living without pain.**

Perhaps that may never happen, but you, as an individual should not have to live with pain. Believing that allows for the opening which may come, to alleviate your suffering.

What Can We Acknowledge?

Having acknowledged our pain we can then discover what it is that causes the pain and why it should endure so. With physical and emotional pain we are injured by something - often more powerful than us.

We need to allow ourselves to go through the stages of grief which give us permission to put the experience in a truer perspective. This again gives us a sense of self worth because we can feel the emotions of grief - and make them comprehensible in our lives.

Our grief because of our pain tells us that we may:

- initially go through a period of shock, sometimes very intense, often numbing

- identify what it is that has hurt us

- discover who, what and why it has hurt us

- consider how much pain is real in relation to our other life experiences

- have time to mourn and adjust to life because of the pain we have felt

---

Usually, when we are in pain, something else is controlling us.

It may be a person, circumstances or a medical condition which takes over. Giving birth is often one of the greatest pains a human being has to endure. And yet, look at the end result. The uterus takes over and expels the child.

There is nearly always a function to pain.

Searching for the reason for your own pain helps make sense of it.

It could:

- alert you to danger

- remind you to never want to experience that again

- be a new start

- or an ending

When we grieve in an open and healthy way we let ourselves know that we have lost something. Something has changed.

It cannot be the same again.

Losing

We are disabled often when we lose that which we have relied upon.

We are disabled when that which is important to us is taken from us, or never given in the first place.

With pain comes loss.
What have you lost?

Finding the answer to this may be very excruciating indeed, but can validate your self worth.

If you want to mend and heal, asking this question is the first step.

'I have lost a limb - it is no longer there'

'I have lost my womb - it was taken from me by an inexperienced gynaecologist'

'I have lost my hearing in an accident'

'I have lost my childhood through being so often raped'

'I have lost my stability because of extreme distress'

'I have lost my mother through death'

'I have lost my sister because of an argument'

'I never received the education to compete for a job - I have lost opportunities'

'I lost my self esteem when I was made insignificant as a lesbian'.

Reasoning

Inherent in some of these statements is also an identifying of the cause of the pain. If we understand the cause we can put reason to it, and then we can go further and live out other important feelings.

What happened?

* **I was completely innocent, somebody else damaged me**

    The girl being raped by her father is innocent. She did nothing to incur such vicious and brutal treatment.

* **I was completely innocent, an accident occurred through bad luck and natural causes**

    The landslide swept me and the house away - no one could have imagined it would happen.

- **I did something to cause this damage**

    I smoked all my life and now I have lung cancer.

Reasoning out what happened puts a framework around our feelings.

The problem for many of us is that we as women are asked too often to share the burden of guilt, when in fact we are innocent. So often it is alleged: "the girl 'led him on'. She was provocative and therefore her father raped her."

Also, we can have horrible, lingering sensations of our own undoing and underneath it all eternally question ourselves, 'If only I'd not .... If only I had ...'

Getting Angry

Coming to grips with the cause of our loss will often prompt our feeling very, very angry indeed.

It is a well recognised part of the grieving process and our taking on board the strength of our anger enables us to express it as a healthy means of overcoming the sense of helplessness we were initially feeling.

Our anger is so very important.

Misdirected anger will continue to damage and hurt other people and we have all been guilty of that.

- Being humiliated by a bus conductor on the way home and then taking it out on the kids is misdirected anger.

Channelled anger first perceives the causes of pain in all its complexity and then does something for the future.

- Wanting to 'get our own back' or punishing the offender could fall into this category.

Constructively channelled anger often tries to stop repetition of the same pain for others.

- Losing someone close because of cancer may motivate us to campaign against cancer causing agents.

Perhaps the most insidious form of anger is that directed against ourselves. It is extremely self destructive. We can watch people nearly wilt away as they again and again inflict their anger upon themselves.

It can make us carry on repeating painful experiences as a way of further punishing ourselves.

Unless we acknowledge and give reason to our pain we won't understand why we have so much anger.

Anger can be very powerful.

Used negatively it is excessively destructive. Often we are angry with 'soft targets' the ones who we know will get as hurt as we've been. Using our techniques for managing distress we realise that the best thing to do with that sort of anger is STOP.

Look And Listen

Looking at the cause of your pain, letting yourself feel what it is that's right and wrong about it, being angry, allows the next step. You can listen to your own sense of judgement about what is best to happen next.

> **If you want to move on and if you've given yourself the chance to really grieve the injustice of your pain (however it was caused) you can LET GO of it.**

You can let it disappear as if it has gone through you and OUT OF YOU. There is, after all, no point in harbouring old wounds which you may have been nurturing to remain open.

There is a weird human experience of 'sweet suffering'. We utter the exclamation, 'Good Grief!'

Why should this be? Do we have to have suffering in our lives to remind us we are alive? Is it that it reminds us of our feelings in a society which so often deadens and dampens real human experience - those powerful emotions which can motivate? Is it that we are encouraged into these spirals so that we persist in keeping ourselves down?

There IS a way out of all this.

Our Healing

Slowly, but surely, we are designed to heal.

They say time is the greatest healer. It is especially so if you have been able to grieve for your loss, acknowledge your self worth and identify why there was loss.

Some pain, some loss, we know will always affect us. The loss of part of our body is irretrievable. Death is final.

> **But, we who live can be part of the life-giving process.**
>
> **Healing is part of that process.**

Once we have let go of those traumatic and energising feelings of grief, suffering and anger we can turn to other forms of emotion, equally powerful, equally energising.

We know that we may never be the same again, but within creativity there are always opportunities to work around loss. We can search for new ways, new people, new ideas and new challenges.

Realising

Usually, during the grieving period we come to the point when we have to face up to what has happened.

> **This moment is the one we dread the most, the time when the final awful truth overwhelms us and grips us like a vice.**

It can be quite a physical reaction; our whole body seems to work as a unit and everything about our being is crystal clear.

> **Perhaps it is reassuring to understand (even if hard to believe) that this moment comes when you *are* ready for it. If the whole body is working as an entity it won't allow you to take this realisation on board until you are prepared.**

That is why we can successfully deny some truths for many years - forever if necessary. It is an important and simple mechanism of survival. If we are still living with the effects or causes of our pain we may not be ready to face the truth. It may be extremely undermining. It is why we can be so very defensive.

> **We live in a dangerous world and it is alright to protect ourselves.**

Even so, the moment of dawning, when it does come, can be like the beginning of a new era. Suddenly, you have shuddered with the reality, as distasteful and distressing as it is. Then, through the course of reasoning and questioning you might discover how it could have been.

There are two alternatives:

1. If you conclude that there were good reasons for it to have been different:

    - It didn't HAVE to have been like that

    - I didn't HAVE to have suffered

    You can then learn from your experience and protect yourself in the future, if at all possible. At this point it is very constructive to seek help, from a friend, or any trusted person.

    If that is unavailable look to yourself as your best friend, one who will learn and grow for the future. One who can be tough and resilient. If that is impossible you may still need to grieve more.

    You may still need to weep and scream and argue.

2. However, if you conclude that there was no way anything could have been different:

    - the death was final

    - no one could have stopped me losing my sight

- it was a freak accident

then the time has come to start, maybe only tentatively, to think about the future.

Accepting

The moment of realisation brings with it an incredible sense of personal armoury which is in no way metallic or rigid. It is fluid and intangible and yet extraordinarily strengthening.

You have found for yourself what it was.

The gnawing which could so easily turn to bitterness can be eradicated.

Suddenly, a burden may feel as if it has lifted. It was a load so great that it weighed you down. You MAY let it go.

Being able to accept the hurts and pains gives us the reason to be able.

It is done. It is gone.

Now I must live for the future.

I want to choose to live.

Our Learning To Become Able

Growing And Developing

Once we have chosen to fight, even what may seem to be the odds against us, we have decided to live with, around and through the disabilities we have suffered.

There is a balance between having deep knowledge and understanding of the damage and its effects on the one hand. On the other there is an acceptance which can put it aside so that we may carry on regardless.

Finding new ways of being active.

Searching for resources to use in a fresh and more efficient manner.

Expecting people around you to respect the differences you have, as you do theirs.

Putting aside self deprecation because of your disability.

These are reminders of wanting to MOVE ON.

It is a constant and never ending battle. Waking each morning with limited mobility is a daily challenge which asks us these fundamental questions:

Do I want to move?

Do I want to make the effort?

Am I worth the struggle?

You have energy.

Something in you can move.

Movement brings change.

Change brings new opportunities.

Becoming Able To The Level Of Our Ability

We have the right to define the level at which we wish to operate in this world.

If we do not want to become strong and mighty, we do not have to. If we want to have a go at running or wheeling the London Marathon then we could start training and make the attempt.

When we have learnt sufficiently about the way our bodies work, in conjunction with our emotional needs, we are in a good place to decide our best level of functioning. You can decide whether you wish to keep 'gently' fit, very fit or super fit. You can also decide to be 'unfit'.

> **Through a process of learning about how your body works in all its complexity you can make informed choices about the way you care for your body.**

Then you can allow your body to take you places you may adventurously want to go.

It is all too often the 'I can't' syndrome. We do have to examine where those words initially came from before adopting them as our own.

The woman with multiple mobility disabilities will have been told she cannot 'play football'. And yet, even slight movement in the legs will allow a game to be played.

- How?

    By one or more people sitting in chairs and passing the ball to each other via the feet. Those with full movement in their legs can play this game and they could also be restricted by keeping the thighs attached to the chair!

    As skills develop, new challenges can be made up. Like creating a goal area or placing the seats at different angles.

    The many variations depend on our imagination.

> **Choosing how skillful you want to become is essential in feeling and being comfortable with our continuously learning to become able.**

Gaining Back Control

Recommended Reading

A Death In The Family
Jean Richardson   A Lion Guide   1982

Beyond Grief
Carol Staudacher   Souvenir Press   1988

Just Like A Girl: How girls learn to be women
Sue Sharpe   Penguin   1976

A Wealth Of Experience: The lives of older women
Susan Hemmings   Pandora Press   1985

Finding A Voice: Asian women in Britain
Amrit Wilson   Virago   1979

In My Own Name: An autobiography
Sharon-Jeet Shan   Womens Press   1985

The Heart Of The Race: Black women's lives in Britain
Beverley Bryan, Stella Dadzie, Suzanne Scafe   Virago   1986

Able Lives: Women's experience of paralysis
Jenny Morris (Ed)   The Women's Press   1989

Love And Pain
Sandra Horley   London: Beford Square Press   1988

The Lesbian Relationship Handbook
Phyllis Athey and Mary Jo Osterman, PUSH   1984

Our Right To Love: A Lesbian resource book
Ginny Vida   Prentice - Hall   1978

Young Gay And Proud
Sasha Alyson   Alyson Publications   1980

The Hite Report
Shere Hite   Summit/Hamlyn   1977

Sex For Women - Who want to have fun and loving relationships with equals
Carmen Kerr   Grove Press   1977

A Womans Place (A guide for women facing divorce)
Sue Witherspoon
Obtain from: **SHAC**
London Housing Aid Centre. 189a Old Brompton Rd London SW5 0AR

Divorce And Your Children
Anne Hooper   Allen and Unwin   1983

Someone To Talk To Directory
Mental Health Foundation   1985

Fit For The Future: The Guide for women who want to live well
Jeanette Winterson   Pandora   1986

Disability Now
Monthly Magazine £10.00 per year
Spastics Society, Freepost 17, London W1E 3HU

Organisations

CRUSE (Organisation for widows)
126 Sheen Road, Richmond, Surrey, TW9 1UR

National Association Of Widows
54 - 57 Allison Street, Digbeth, Birmingham, B5 5TH.

Gay Bereavement Project
Unitarian Rooms, Hoop Lane, London, NW11 8BS.

Disabled Living Foundation
380/384, Harrow Road, London, W9 2HU. Tel 071-289 6111

Disability Alliance
25 Denmark St London WC2 8NJ Tel 071 240 0806

British Council Of Organisations Of Disabled People
St Mary's Church, Greenlaw St, Woolwich, London SE18 5AR

Women With Visible And Invisible Disabilities
Kings Cross Womens Centre, 71 Tonbridge St, London WC1H 9DZ Tel 071 837 7509

Standing Conference Of Ethnic Minority Senor Citizens
5a Westminster Bridge Rd London SE1 7XW Tel 071 928 0095

National Council For Carers And Elderly Dependents Ltd
29, Chilworth Mews, London, W2 3RG. Tel 071-262 1451

Age Concern
Bernard Sunley House, 60 Pitcairn Rd, Mitcham Surrey CR4 3LL Tel 081 640 5431

Equal Opportunities Commission
Overseas House, Quay Street, Manchester, M3 3HN. Tel 061 833 9244

Institute Of Race Relations
2 - 6 Leeke St, London WC1X 9HS Tel 071 837 0041

Asian Womens Resource Centre
134 Minet Ave, London NW10 Tel 081 961 5701

Claudia Jones Organisation
Advice and Support Centre for Afro Caribbean Women
103 Stoke Newington Rd, London N16 8BX   Tel 071 241 1646

Incest Survivors In Strength
23 Tunstall Rd, Brixton, London SW9

Survivors Of Child Abuse
18 Denmark Rd, Gloucester GL1 5HZ Tel 0452 309026

Incest Crisis Line
66 Marriott Close, Bedfont, Feltham, Middx Tel 081 890 4732

Mothers Of Abused Children
Tel 0965 31432

Black Lesbian And Gay Centre Project
BM 4390, London WC1N 3XX Tel 081 885 3543

GEMMA
For lesbians concerned with disabilities BM Box 5700 London

Lesbian Employment Rights
Room 203, Southbank House, Black Prince Rd, London SE1 7SJ   Tel 071 587 1636

CHAPTER 12
TAKING RESPONSIBILITY

We have considered many aspects and dimensions of self-empowerment in this book. To live actively and constructively with the knowledge of our personal powers is to live with, and understand, our responsibilities. It is also to challenge how responsibility has been taken FROM us and how we can become TOO responsible.

In this final chapter we shall return to the model used in the first chapter on page 4 to distinguish the physically and emotionally assertive woman, in relation to her responsibilities. Before this however, we will:

Define responsibility

> **Question ownership**

>> **Examine what TAKING responsibility means**

Defining Responsibility

Responsibility is about:

> *Responding* to a need for activity

>> Having a certain *involvement* with the activity

>>> *Caring* about the consequences and anticipating them

>>>> *Assuming and assessing our power* over that for which we have responsibility

The relationship between these four features is a dynamic one.

So, we act with responsibility when for instance we:

> *Respond* to our children's need to be fed

>> *Involve* ourselves in feeding them

>>> *Care* about the consequences of feeding

>>>> *Assume and assess our power* to feed or not to feed.

Questioning Ownership

If we are responsible for something we often assume a certain amount of 'ownership' of it.

"I am responsible for *my* child; *my* home; *my* body; *my* job."

We can question the concept of ownership because we can ask:

"How much control and power do I have over my area of responsibility?

Is it a *shared* control or power?

Is it only a *token* of control and power?"

So:

I have power and control over my young child.

Do I share any of that power and control - with for instance:
>   The child?
>   My partner?
>   Her grandparents?
>   The Education Authority?
>   The Health Service?

Do I only have a token of power because the Social Services Department have assumed responsibility for her?

So, again:

I have power and control over my job - but HOW MUCH?

Do I share any of my power and control - with for instance other colleagues?

Do I only have a token of power because I was appointed to do an impossible job and the boss is controlling everything I do ?

It would then be more accurate to suggest that:

This is *my* job only in title.

If, however you have complete power and control over the activity of your work then it would be right to suggest that it is *your* job.

If we now add together the dimensions of ownership and responsibility two questions are raised:

1.   Over what do I have the right to assume ownership?

2.   Over what do I assume the right to have responsibility?

Returning to our definition of responsibility may help clarify our thinking:

Why do we *respond* to the need for activity?

Why are we *involved* in the activity?

Why do we *care?*

Why do we assume and assess our *power?*

Can we then say:

I own my child because I respond to her need for me?

I own my child because I am involved in her survival?

I own my child because I care about her?

I own my child because I have assumed and assessed my power and control over her?

But of course nobody owns their child so ownership in this sense sounds harsh, inhumane and bizarre, and yet some parents do subscribe to this form of ownership of their children.

> **It is important therefore, to:**
>
> 1. Recognise our MOTIVES in wishing to own
>
> 2. Understand how we rely on our PRIVILEGE to own something.

So, if we acknowledge shared ownership, instead of full ownership as the above suggests, then we are allowing the child her own personhood, within her own context of life.

It becomes evident then, that parenting a child is not necessarily about "MY responsibilities for MY child", but much more an acceptance of the bestowal of RIGHTS that go with your power and influence over the child.

"I am responding to this child and care about her. I have assumed some power and control over her. She has rights and I have rights as her parent or guardian. I am a custodian of her life until she is old enough to decide her own future."

It could be argued that we own only the rights that go with our ownership.

Money is normally the method of defining ownership in this consumerist society. Money gives us a 'right to purchase'.

● Some desperate western people are even purchasing the adoption of children from poorer nations. They then assume responsibilities for the child, in relation to the rights endowed by society.

We might even add, perhaps cynically, that once we have assumed ownership of something we can then do what we like with it, so long as it is within the limits imposed by society. These limits may or may not be helpful.

- So, for instance if we own our car, our power is such that it can be lethal if we drive carelessly. The law informs us of our choices in how to drive the car within the limits of the Highway Code. If we are reckless our USE of the car can be restricted, so that it can become a USELESS item if we are unable to drive it - even if we still 'own' it. Our power is taken away from us.

What then, might we consider our fundamental rights of ownership in life? The ownership of that which is truly ours?

Should we ever be expected to have full ownership rights over:

Other people?

Other objects?

However, we can expect to have full ownership rights over:

Our body

Our emotions

Our attitudes

Our abilities

Our knowledge

Ownership assumes power and control over that which we own.

Responsibility assumes that we acknowledge our response, our involvement, our care for consequences and our level of power and control.

Ownership and responsibility are socially constructed concepts, which are used to define boundaries of behaviour.

Under a patriarchal and capitalist influence these concepts have become distorted to fit the interests of the ruling groups.

"I am allowed to own (through my purchasing power) all these goods, materials, space and energy. I am also allowed to own people because I have the ability to pay them and they are dependent on me."

It is then unfortunately too often the case that such powerful people do not take responsibility for the effects of their power. So, what does TAKING responsibility mean?

Taking Responsibility

Taking responsibility asks us to be active in using our power. It assumes that we can use our power to further our interests of responding, involving and caring. We also acknowlege that we have some influence over the situation we are in.

The problem however, is that we may take too little responsibility, in which case we short measure our own capacity to be powerfully responsible people. We may then allow other, more powerful people to control us.

Or, we can take too much responsibility which means we are unnecessarily working too hard to respond or be involved or care. It can also often mean that we take away other people's responsibilities and also perhaps their power.

When we TAKE responsibility a decision of some sort is usually made.

Consciously or unconsciously we question further the form our responsibility will take:

225   Gaining Back Control

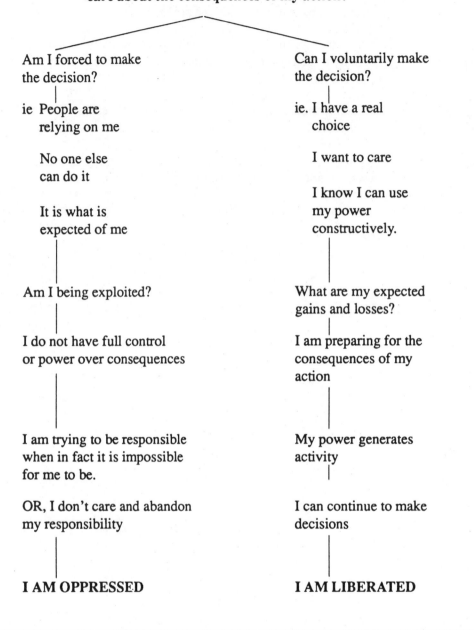

A DECISION HAS TO BE MADE

**Will I respond, be involved and
care about the consequences of my action?**

Am I forced to make the decision?	Can I voluntarily make the decision?
ie People are relying on me	ie. I have a real choice
No one else can do it	I want to care
It is what is expected of me	I know I can use my power constructively.
Am I being exploited?	What are my expected gains and losses?
I do not have full control or power over consequences	I am preparing for the consequences of my action
I am trying to be responsible when in fact it is impossible for me to be.	My power generates activity
OR, I don't care and abandon my responsibility	I can continue to make decisions
I AM OPPRESSED	**I AM LIBERATED**

**The diagram illustrates the questions we can ask
when we are making decisions about our responsibility.**

It implies that we weigh up the factors and influences involved when we make a decision so that we can live with our understanding of our real choices and power - or lack of them. It also enables us to identify how and why we are so often forced, particularly as women, to take on responsibilities which are not really ours.

Then, irritatingly, we are blamed for things going wrong because we were expected to be responsible - but we did not have the real power to make it right.

> **This IS blaming the victim.**

Frequently we take on so much responsibility because we care too much and are very aware of consequences, especially if things go wrong.

So, for instance we end up cleaning the house because we know that insanitary conditions will be unhealthy. If we live with other people who do not see the need to clean, do not care and certainly don't want to be involved in doing it, we do the cleaning and this results in our taking on their responsibilities.

This then takes us back to our fundamental assertiveness rights which are to challenge others to think about and accept their responsibilities. Making others understand and accept their responsibilities could relate to anything from a personal relationship imbalance to challenging the government for not taking enough responsibility for the consequences of its power and control over us.

Such a form of behaviour accepts that we are truly accountable to each other, as well as to ourselves because:

> **as assertive women we are searching for an equilibrium of control where both parties feel and own their personal sense of control.**

This behaviour allows for people to move on, and for people to generate new activity because previous consequences have been understood and accounted for.

This behaviour can be defined as:

> **EXERCISING POWER WITH INTEGRITY**

If we acknowledge that we do have power we then take part in a constant battle to 'make the right decisions'. We would not be human if we were to fulfill this notion! Life might even become boring! However, we can use our power with integrity.

> **In other words:**
>
> - we can search for the effects our power has on ourselves and others
>
> - we can make as much of an honest appraisal as we can *especially* when we have an advantage of power
>
> - we can enjoy a sense of completion in using our power effectively
>
> - we can own our feelings, emotions and physical abilities

Taking responsibility truly *defines* our *activity* in the world.

USING OUR ENERGY ⟶ PROVIDES MOVEMENT ⟶ MAKES AN ACTION

ENERGY = MOVEMENT = ACTION = POWER

We are usually far more powerful than we think ourselves to be.

> **To own our ability to be potentially powerful is to live with a truth which no one can take from us.**

After all it is in the interests of ruling groups to contain our powers because then we will not challenge them. These powerful people do not have regard for our personal ownership rights.

> **Taking power without regard for the consequences to others is the opposite of taking responsibility.**
>
> **There is no care or concern for the welfare and self empowerment of others.**
>
> **There is only care for a self-interested gain which may be taken at the expense of others.**
>
> **If we take the products of poorer nations at vastly under-valued prices, we take power at their expense and we have no regard for the consequences of our taking.**

We have re-considered sources of power in this book. We have examined methods, ideas and strategies for developing our powers.

> **There is only one thing in this life that we can truly take responsibility for and that is OURSELVES.**

If we look again at the vision of the physically and emotionally assertive woman we can stop to consider what responsibilities come with it.

The Physically And Emotionally Assertive Woman

The physically and emotionally assertive woman is one who desires awareness, strength and a 'whole personhood'.

She seeks knowledge to further her understanding of her own emotions and physical power. She acknowledges her ability as a means of demonstrating her attitude towards herself, others and her use of resources.

She is conscious of how she makes decisions and the effect her power has on herself and others.

The Vision Translated In Terms Of Responsibility

I am my body, so therefore I own it and can make decisions about whether to take responsibility for it:

I want to respond to my body

I want to be involved consciously in the work and functioning of my body

I want to care for my body and anticipate consequences of that caring

I want to assume and assess the physical power I have

I am my emotions, so therefore I own them and can make decisions about whether to take responsibility for them:

I want to respond to my emotions

I want to be involved in the effects they have on me and others

I want to care for my emotions and my emotional stability and be aware of the consequences

I want to assume and assess the emotional power I have

I am my abilities, so therefore I own them and can make decisions about whether to take responsibility for my ability, or lack of ability:

I want to respond to my abilities

I want to be involved in the experience of using my abilities

I want to care about the level of my ability

I want to assume and assess the powers my abilities give me

I am my attitudes, so therefore I own them and can make decisions about whether to take responsibility for my attitudes:

I want to respond to my attitudes because they define the decisions I make in my life

I want to be involved in how my attitudes affect myself and others

I want to care about my attitudes

I want to assume and assess the power that my attitudes give me

I am a strong, aware and whole woman, so therefore I am my own woman:

I want to be be responsive to myself and my needs

I want to be involved in my whole personhood

I want to care about myself and the consequences of my actions

I want to assume and assess my power and I can use it to protect my own self esteem and the self esteem of others.

Gaining Back Control

We are already powerful women.

We respond all day to demands, stresses, adventures and hopes.

We are inexplicably bound up in each other, in our society and cultures and in the world as a whole.

People depend on us and we satisfy their needs interminably. We are so often in control of that process, and yet our feelings of powerlessness can come about because others, more powerful, dominate us and use us.

Each time we strengthen our ownership of ourselves as physically and emotionally assertive women we give ourselves opportunities to gain back control.

Through assuming our power and the dignity of exercising it with integrity we challenge our previous position of oppression.

We may be beaten down by the oppressor over and over again and yet:

we gain back control through finding new ways
of challenging and new ways of expecting equality
and value in human relationships.

Rise up and go forward like an amazon reclaiming her own territory.

Gaining Back Control

Women and Power

Notes

1. Carol Anne Davis "On living with the panic of agoraphobia" EVERYWOMAN p. 20 April 1989

2. Information from an article by Joy Melville "Frantic slaves to a life of fear". SUNDAY TIMES (New Society) 4.6.89

3. Isaac Marks "Living With Fear" McGraw Hill 1989

4. Susan Griffin "Made From This Earth" p. 263 Womens Press 1982

5. Ellen Kuzwayo "Call Me Woman" Womens Press 1985

6. Conversation June 1990

7. Health Education Authority "Beating Heart Disease" p. 2 (based on figures from the Office of Population Census and surveys 1987)

8. Anne Dickson "A Woman In Your Own Right" Quartet 1988

9. Ibid. pp 4-8

10. Meg Bond "Stress and Self Awareness. A guide for nurses" pp. 130-1 Heinemann 1990

11. "A Woman in Your Own Right" op. cit p. 29-36

12. Angela Phillips and Jill Rakusen "Our Bodies Ourselves" Penguin 1989

13. H G Q Rowett "Basic Anatomy and Physiology" adapted from Introduction. Murray 1983

14. Angela Phillips and Jill Rakusen "Our Bodies Ourselves" pp. 22 and 26 Penguin 1978

15. "Anatomy for Artists" pp. 5 No. 4 Leonardo Collections Il Prisma Editions

16. "WHICH? WAY TO HEALTH" p. 26/7 April 1989

17. "A Guide to the Health and Safety at Work Act 1974" Health and Safety Executive (HS (R)6)

18. Denise Caignon and Gail Groves "Her Wits About Her" Womens Press 1989

19. Judith Lowe and Isabel Wright "Streetwise" Ariel Books pp. 27-33, 44/5, 51, 55, 69, 78/9 198

20. Kaleghl Quinn "Stand Your Ground: A women's guide to self-preservation" MacDonald Optima 1988

21. Penny Gulliver, from her video "Self Defence for Women" Seven Dimensions, Australia 1989

22. Diana Warren-Holland, Denise Russell Jones, Rachel Stewart and Women Against Rape "Self Defence for Women" pp. 113-135 Hamlyn 1987.

APPENDIX I

Protect your Back and Lift It

(From: Weight Training for Women, Mary Southall and E G Bartlett, published by David & Charles)

1. Apparatus

The apparatus you will need for weight training can be as simple or as complex as you like to make it, and will in part be dictated by how much money you are prepared to spend. You can manage with a pair of dumb-bells, but it is better if you can also add a barbell and a bench, because these will give you a greater variety of exercises to make your training more interesting. Simply repeating the same exercises can become boring and this can sap your resolve to continue. If you want to use expensive machines, it is probably best to begin your training in a leisure centre or commercial gymnasium where this apparatus is available. You can then see how you get on with it before rushing into a large outlay of capital.

Assuming you are planning to train at home and have no apparatus, the first piece to consider buying is a pair of dumb-bells. There are two kinds: those made of metal or heavy plastic of a fixed weight, and those that consist of a short rod with collars that enable you to slip disc weights on to either side, holding them in position by screwing down collars. The latter are better, as they will enable you to increase the weight you are using, as your strength increases, and so will give you progressively increasing resistance to work against - an essential factor if you want to develop muscle. In the early days of weight training, the weights on dumb-bells or barbells consisted of hollow metal spheres into which lead shot could be poured to increase the weight being lifted. Today, there are similar ones into which wet or dry sand can be poured to increase the weight. Since either of these alternatives would involve weighing the dumb-bells to see what weights you were actually lifting, it is better to buy the type in which you simply slide on extra disc weights. These are labelled either in pounds or kilograms, and are so graduated that you can increase the weight you are using by as little as 1 lb or 1/2 kg.

The next piece of equipment you should consider buying is a barbell. This consists of a bar, approximately 5 or 6 ft long, with two collars either end which you can screw down to hold disc weights in position. The inner collars are tightly screwed equidistant from either end and about 6 in from the ends. Disc weights are then slipped on to make up the desired weight. The outer collars are now added to hold these weights in position, and screwed down tightly. You must of course balance the weight on either side, and make sure that the collars are firm, so that the weights will not slide inwards to trap your hands, or fall off on your toes.

Often dumb-bells and barbells are sold together as a set. The disc weights with them will fit either the barbell rod or the dumb-bell rods. The cost is dictated by the total poundage you buy. You can get sets as low as 50 lb or go up to several hundred pounds. It is best to start with the lower range and then buy more weights as you need them. If your rods are of a standard thickness, this is easy, but be wary because some manufacturers have made their rods of a slightly different thickness so that only their weights will fit them. This limits you to going back to the same firm for extra discs. Although pounds are used in this book, some firms are labelling their weights in kilograms. If you are using kilograms it is simple to make the necessary conversions.

The cost of even such simple apparatus as described above can be as much as £1 per 1lb weight, but second-hand sets can often be seen in the body-building magazines or in Exchange and Mart and of course these are just as good, but make sure before you buy anything that the collars fit and grip tightly, and that they are not rusty. Collars tighten by screwing down a peg or by using an Alan key.

To add further variety to the exercises you can do at home, consider next getting a bench. This can be a simple flat bench about 18 ins. from the floor, long enough to support your buttocks, back, head and shoulders, with your feet on the floor off one end. An ordinary wooden household bench is quite serviceable; if you want something more elaborate, padded ones of tubular steel are available in sports shops, as are adjustable ones which enable the top to be set at various angles.

With these three pieces of apparatus, you are ready to start home training, but even if you have only got dumb-bells, do not worry, because you will see in Chapters 10 and 11 that for every barbell exercise there is a corresponding one with dumb-bells, so you can easily make substitutions in your routines and develop the same muscles.

If you want to add further to your home equipment, the next purchase is a pair of iron boots. These are metal plates which you strap to the soles of your own shoes, and they have a rod projecting either side, to which you can fit disc weights, holding them in position with a screw collar as you do on the dumb-bells. Thus you can add to the weight on your feet when doing exercises for leg or abdominal development. Heavy boots would be a good substitute if you do not wish to buy the iron ones.

A wrist roller is another useful piece of equipment. This is a short rod usually of wood with a cord attached to the centre. On this cord you hang weights, and you turn the rod to wind them up by the cord. It is such a simple design that you could make one for yourself out of a piece of broomstick 1 ft long.

Many people today turn to rowing machines or exercise bikes for their work-outs. The rowing machine consists of a sliding seat, a foot rest and two handles which you pull against the resistance of springs in a simulation of a rowing boat. It exercises the same muscles as rowing on a lake or on the sea would do. The exercise bike is really a static bicycle. You sit on the saddle, hold the handlebars and pedal, the resistance of the pedals, which is adjustable, providing the exercise. These bikes have a resistance indicator, a timer and a speed meter to show how fast you are going. It is usual to cycle for a set time against a set resistance, and to increase either the time or the resistance or both as you progress. The benefits are similar to cycling, and you have to balance the absence of traffic hazards against the fact that you list the advantages of being in the open air and getting somewhere.

If you decide to train at a leisure centre, you may find that they give you the option of using loose weights on dumb-bell and barbell rods such as we have described above, but you are more likely to find that they have machines. These have the advantage that the weights cannot fall out and injure you since they move on runners, and you can change the weight you are using more easily, since you simply insert a pin at the weight level that you want. The machines generally found at leisure centres or commercial gyms are called 'Stations', and you will normally find the following fifteen stations:

1   Leg Press Station, This is a padded seat with a back rest, on a metal bar. It has resistance foot rests attached to an adjustable weight stack.

2   Hip Flexor Station, A steel frame with a padded back, arm supports and hand grips. It is fitted at a suitable height to allow floor clearance when you are supported on your forearms.

3   Thigh and Knee Leg Extension Station, A padded bench with foot rollers connected to an adjustable weight stack.

4   High Pulley Station, A curved bar with handgrips, connected by cable to a high pulley and weight stack.

5   Rowing Station, A weight stack attached to low cables and stirrup handles. It has a padded seat and foot rests.

6   Low Pulley Thigh Pulls Station, A foot strap and cable attached to a floor level pulley and weight stack.

7   Dead Lift Station, An arrangement of weights on runners attached to the wall, with handles to raise.

8   Abdominal Conditioner Sit-ups Station, A padded board adjustable to several angles, with foot rollers.

9   Chest Press Station, A padded bench or stool, with metal lifting arm and hand grips attached to a weight stack.

10   Chest Bench Station, A seat with arm resistance pads at shoulder height, attached to an adjustable weight stack.

11   Leg Squat Station, This consists of two shoulder pads attached to a resistance lifting bar and adjustable weight stack.

12   Dipping Station, A low metal support with rail and hand grips.

13   Chinning Station, A high metal support, with rail and hand grips.

14   Standing Twister, A circular turntable platform, attached to a handrail at shoulder height.

15   Seated Twister, A circular turntable seat with a foot rest attached to a waist level handrail.

Sometimes, several of these machines will be incorporated in one piece of apparatus, standing centrally, and you will be able to move around it, doing one exercise on one side and another on another. Such multi-gyms, as they are called, can also be bought for home use, but they are rather expensive and of course they take up a considerable amount of room.

As well as leisure centres run by local authorities, there are an increasing number of commercial gyms. Most of these are very well equipped, and as well as all the apparatus listed above they will have showers, saunas and other extras. Before joining one, however, it would be wise to pay a visit to see how it is being run. Is there a qualified instructor in attendance? If so, will you have to follow a set course which she or he prescribes? Is instruction on an individual or class basis?

To get the best out of weight training, individual courses need to be prescribed for your individual needs. You may not get this in a class. You need an instructor in whom you have confidence and with whom you get on well. Find out all these things before you commit yourself.

APPENDIX II

WOMEN'S SELF DEFENCE

JUDITH LOWE
(ILEA ADVISORY LECTURER: WOMEN'S SELF DEFENCE/ADULT EDUCATION
AND THE YOUTH SERVICE)

This is a brief and sometimes rather personal account of the history of Self Defence in the
ILEA, the progress we have made, the issues involved in the teaching of this complex and
demanding subject and a look at the present context in which we teach.

The acceptance of Women's Self Defence into the ILEA happened in the Autumn of 1981.
Since then the curriculum has developed and become more sophisticated and we have
devised and run our own tutor training programmes. Now, apart from the shortage of
teachers, we are able to offer a wide variety of courses as individuals within the teachers'
group have acquired specialist knowledge and experience.

The original London Women's Self Defence Group in its pre-ILEA days was largely
composed of the members of a Women's Karate Club, taught by Joan Baxter at the
Women's Arts Alliance. This was in '78, '79, '80. Many of us also joined a mixed club out
at Plaistow and took our gradings there. Most of us were at that time involved in the
various compaigns around violence against women. Several were workers with Women's
Aid, others of us were part of the Women against Violence against Women movement. The
interest and commitment to self defence grew out of the women's politics of the time and
the growing awareness of the scale of the problem.

When a few months ago a police leaflet on personal safety landed on my mat I was
interested to see how respectable the idea of women's safety has become. The leaflet offers
the whole range of crisis lines and clearly endorses the women's refuges which it
mentions. Ten years ago, violence against women was still considered a bit of a joke. Any
mention of domestic violence was consistently greeted with cries for refuges for 'poor
men'. A guardsman was let off a rape charge on the grounds that it could ruin his career -
hence the huge graffiti across the Mall, the first of many 'actions' in this era to contest the
acceptability or invisibility of violence against women both on the streets and in their own
homes. These years saw a growing rise in the amount of activity by various groups of
women - the Reclaim the Night Marches, the 'Take your Hands off My Body' stickers, the
campaigns against the pornography industrty and the representations of women in the
media which were insulting to women, thereby promoting violence and abuse against us.
Also there were the growing number of Rape Crisis groups and then the Incest Survivors
Movement. Again it's hard to recall at this distance how derided and ignored these issues
were at the time. I remember a friend of mine in an Incest group saying 'Just you wait,
child abuse is going to be the big thing in a few years time...' There were arson attacks on
porn shops, paint bombs thrown at cinema screens, the 'Angry Women' graffiti, and links
being made between women's power and position in society and the everyday violence
that they faced.

No less significant were the ever increasing attacks on the Black communities in London
and the threat posed by the resurgence of openly fascist political organisations like the
National Front. As an increasingly racially mixed group we were committed to a

perspective in self defence in which an analysis of racist violence and harassment was essential. Over the years we have committed ourselves to developing techniques for confronting racism in the classroom, challenging racist attitudes in a white student group, supporting and protecting Black students from racist comments and behaviour in a group, and supporting and encouraging the emergence of Black women only classes where Black women could freely define and develop their own self defence curriculum. Again as a brief historical aside, I remember us meeting up as a group to march together on the New Cross Fire demonstration.

I mention all these things because I want to set the beginnings of Women's Self Defence in a political context, next to and part of the other developments in Women's Education. It is important because, seen from this perspective, the curriculum for this subject cannot solely be a physical one but has to address both the politics of violence and oppression and the feelings and experiences of women.

I can't, here, give a full account of every possible contributory factor but I want to place Women's Self Defence as a radical initiative of its time. I recall the tremendous excitement of those first few years of teaching. As a group we met often and trained together and compared notes on teaching. In the classes it felt like we were doing something incredibly daring just by being there. We were beginning to define our own demands around our safety and well-being and beginning to challenge the power of the batterer, rapist and abuser of women.

In 1981 at the suggestion of Amanda Wooley, then with the WEA, I began teaching a class at Battersea Arts Centre funded by the WEA. I taught this class as the practical part of a weekly women's day on issues around violence. The afternoon class, a reading, study and discussion class, was taught by Sheila Jeffreys. Most of our classes until then had been informally organised through women's groups and personal contacts. Amanda and I wrote a paper on Women's Self Defence explaining the approach that was being developed - that is, away from martial arts towards a class that would also involve discussion and the validation of skills and options other than physical fighting. We sent our proposal to Stan Woolhem of the P.E. College and he was keen to back-up our proposals.
Clapham/Battersea hosted a conference for all interested ILEA personnel and there we met Janet Paraskeva Hunt from the Inspectorate who instantly gave us her approval and full back-up. I taught a pilot course for the ILEA; we started having training days for the teachers and finally the first validation weekend for the group who had already been training and teaching for some time. Women's Self Defence, as we had defined it, became part of the ILEA provision for Adult Education and the Youth Service.

Janet Paraskeva Hunt helped us put together a budget to run a training programme for new teachers and we ran the second Training Course. To date we have completed the fourth with the support and encouragement of Valerie Hider, Staff Inspector.

Also in those early years, we met and took part in some workshops led by Kaleghl Quinn, author of Stand Your Ground and a few years ago we were able to add some of her trained teachers to the ILEA list. This included Chris Lepley who tragically died last year. Isabel Wright and myself wrote the BBC book 'Streetwise' and I appeared in the television series. Meiling Jin taught the first Black women's class in Camden, Judith Shaw one of the first classes for young women with learning difficulties. Maria Jastrzebska, also from the original group, is currently the Equal Opportunities Advisory Teacher for Self Defence in

Schools. Many of us taught women from the Greenham camp and looked at some of the techniques of non-violent action. We also scored high in the Looney Left tabloid wars and were mentioned no less than three times in Tory Party Broadcasts for the Islington based Lesbian class. (It was the funding for the gym mats which provoked the notoriety!)

When we came to organise the third Teacher Training Course, Elsie Sharples, who has organised Self Defence in the Borough of Southwark, contacted us and we then met up with Claudia Silva and Carla Drayton. They were part of the Selection Group for that course and have since contributed so much, as Black women teachers; as highly skilled martial artists; and now as teacher trainers from the fourth course. Carla and I made a video with the ILEA Television and Video Unit in which we outline and discuss the key concepts in teaching Women's Self Defence.

Since we started, the syllabus and some of the concerns of the subject have changed in terms of emphasis and sometimes in content. The issues of racism, class, sexuality, and disability have continued to be debated and new material incorporated into the syllabus.

Self Defence is now a major growth industry and unfortunately not very much of it bears up too well under close inspection. There are an awful lot of ex-army types or black belt martial artists who are making small fortunes out of women's fears by offering courses put together without any thought for the feelings and experiences that women have. Neither are they interested in discussion of issues or of affirming the skills that their students already possess. An example of the worst in this field was a television programme in which one of the male 'experts' displayed the merits of his course. It seemed to consist of two basic stages. Firstly he horrified the women on his course with the most vicious stories of women who had been sexually mutilated in an attack and had not fought back. He then used the profound anxiety which he had aroused in them as a basis for pumping up their aggression and violence towards a would be attacker. He taught them a series of extremely unpleasant fighting techniques completely out of context and with no regard whatever for their reservations. His line seemed to be the one of "They're all animals out there and you'll only stand a chance of survival if you are on your guard against everyone, all the time, and then ready to gouge out their eyeballs at the drop of a hat..." One of his students was interviewed before and after and it was clear her peace of mind had been wrecked by this man. She no longer felt able to be trusting towards anyone she didn't know and in fact had become suspicious and frightened of just about everyone.

Of course not all private self defence classes are as ghastly as this. However even some of the best classes fall into the type of offering solutions or 'Golden Rules' to what are in the end, often complex human situations. Also some of these well meaning pieces of advice verge on making us so safe that our lives would be unliveable. We can't always walk along the main roads - some of us live on badly lit side-roads, we can't all go by cab everywhere or in our own cars. In any case, women are attacked in their cars and attacked by cab drivers. Also we're not necessarily safe in our own homes as the statistics on domestic violence demonstrate.

There is often too an amazing conjuring trick played around identifying the agency of violence. I was enormously depressed and angered to hear, after a woman was stabbed to death recently, the police describe the single train carriages, where the attack had taken place, as 'death-traps' and call for their removal. It is an illogicality and serves only to confuse the issues and lead us away from attempting to analyse why our society produces violence of that kind. When a woman was murdered on the motorway, the police fortunately didn't call for all motorways to be out of bounds for women, though they did issue guidelines which have as their basis all the familiar assumptions - "all strangers are potential enemies, don't trust anyone, don't go any where, try never to be alone at any time...women are weak, their judgments are not to be trusted...these attackers are animals, there's nothing you can do to save yourself..."

For me the starting point is to help students rebuild their confidence in themselves, in their own strength, skills and intuition so that they can, without undue anxiety, really take part in life again, and live their lives fully without restriction, taking their own risks according to their own judgments. Also I feel very strongly that the idea that all strangers are dangerous is a deeply destructive one and not to be endorsed by anything that we teach. We want to give our students the feeling that they can enjoy life and be enriched by all kinds of ordinary, benign human contact.

Self Defence should ideally be a subject in which the students are helped to be able to think for themselves, even in difficult and frightening circumstances. We look at how we can encourage the women who come to our classes to be creative and build on the wide variety of skills and experiences which they bring with them to the class. We look at developing good intuition, the use of all inter-personal skills, the deployment of humour, calmness and kindness as well as how to channel fear, anger and aggression. We teach a variety of physical techniques; fighting, avoiding, escaping, using balance and breathing and momentum. This involves understanding the basic principles and being able to adapt and be flexible according to the various requirements of individual students. We encourage students to build on the techniques themselves and create their own unique style of fighting, rather than drilling them through the 'perfect' textbook movement. Again we use the techniques in conjunction with the feelings they bring up. We look at our fears of panicking, of being weak, of being violent ourselves and how we feel about fighting back...does it make it worse? Can we ever really be effective in a physical fight with a man? As well as this we offer the students some techniques for alleviating stress and anxiety and often all kinds of general health and well being issues can be explored in the class. As teachers we are creating experiences and structuring discussions which can nourish our students' sense of self-worth and help them feel that they themselves are able to be resourceful, wise and powerful. We have, over the years developed a response to violence which has a grounding in political analysis and personal counselling and expertise in movement and the use of physical and emotional strength.

At the moment the future is a bit of an unknown. So far as I know, of the London Boroughs, only Southwark has produced its own Teacher Training Course. I designed and taught this Course and it was set up and supported by Elsie Sharples from the Leisure and Recreation Department and Yvonne Korn of the Police and Community Safety Unit, financed by the Women's Committee, and helped out by Southwark A.E.I. Its aim has been to provide Southwark with its own pool of local teachers who can now teach within their own communities and within the local adult provision. Several other Boroughs seem interested in setting up their own scheme and with the forthcoming demise of the ILEA looming, I shall be happy to help out anyone who is contemplating doing something similar.

My main worry is that our work and our years of expertise get diluted and invisibilised as the demand for slick presentation, training packs, easy robotic techniques and instant solutions become more acceptable. Because the thought of being the victim of an attack is so frightening, everyone understandably wants a short cut package of fail safe rules to apply. Unfortunately what works for one person may not work for another. What is useful and progressive in one situation might be bitterly destructive in another. Every piece of self defence is a unique act borne out of a unique human situation. Obviously we can all learn to be aware and reasonably sensible about our own safety, but in the end, some of what happens in an attack will depend on the way we are able to respond to it. It is harder to be with your students, helping them to work out their own strengths, than to produce a shiny set of 'Golden Rules'. It is more exhausting as a teacher to encourage your students to come out with their negative attitudes about their own experiences and abilities and help them deal with them, than to impose a simplistic 'never trust strangers' attitude. As a group we need to still have the energy and cohesion to fight for a Self Defence which takes on our own humanity and our desire to live in a more peaceful and just society.

Finally, I would like to thank all the many people who have contributed over the years to the work we are doing. Firstly, I would like to mention all the lesbians, Black and white, who have been as ever at the forefront of initiating and fighting for women's issues to be taken seriously. I say this not to be controversial but as a matter of historical fact. Then I would like to thank all our various teachers, female and male, for all their skills and encouragement. Thanks too to all our Colleagues in education for their support and of course to all our students who have taught us so much...and lastly 'Good Luck!' to all the Self Defence teachers trying to earn their livings out there...refining and developing their teaching, working with Black women, pensioners, school children, women with disabilities, women in trades unions, mums with toddlers...on council estates, crummy community halls and of course within the A.E.I.'s.

Judith Lowe, 1988

The author is currently devoting energy to the setting up of a Centre in Leicester which would provide a focus to examine our needs as women for well-being, fitness and preventative health care.

The philosophy of the work will be based on all the issues in this book. The intention is to promote the exchange of information and skills which especially attends to our being physically assertive women.

The Aims of the Centre are:

1   To develop knowledge and ability in women who can use their physical presence to protect themselves, control and own their future.

2   For women and girls to feel and know their own strength through understanding and experiencing their bodies and their physical capacity to use resources with confidence.

3   To promote health in women and girls by their holistic understanding of their physical needs which rely on many alternatives in health care and prevention of illness.

4   To continually open avenues of access and information to women of varying racial backgrounds, women with disabilities, lesbians, older and younger women, women of low economic status and women carers.

If you are interested in receiving more information about our work or have any comments or suggestions to make we would be very pleased to hear from you.

Please write to:

Vida Pearson
PAVIC Publications
Sheffield City Polytechnic
36 Collegiate Crescent Sheffield S10 2BP
England